Rainforest

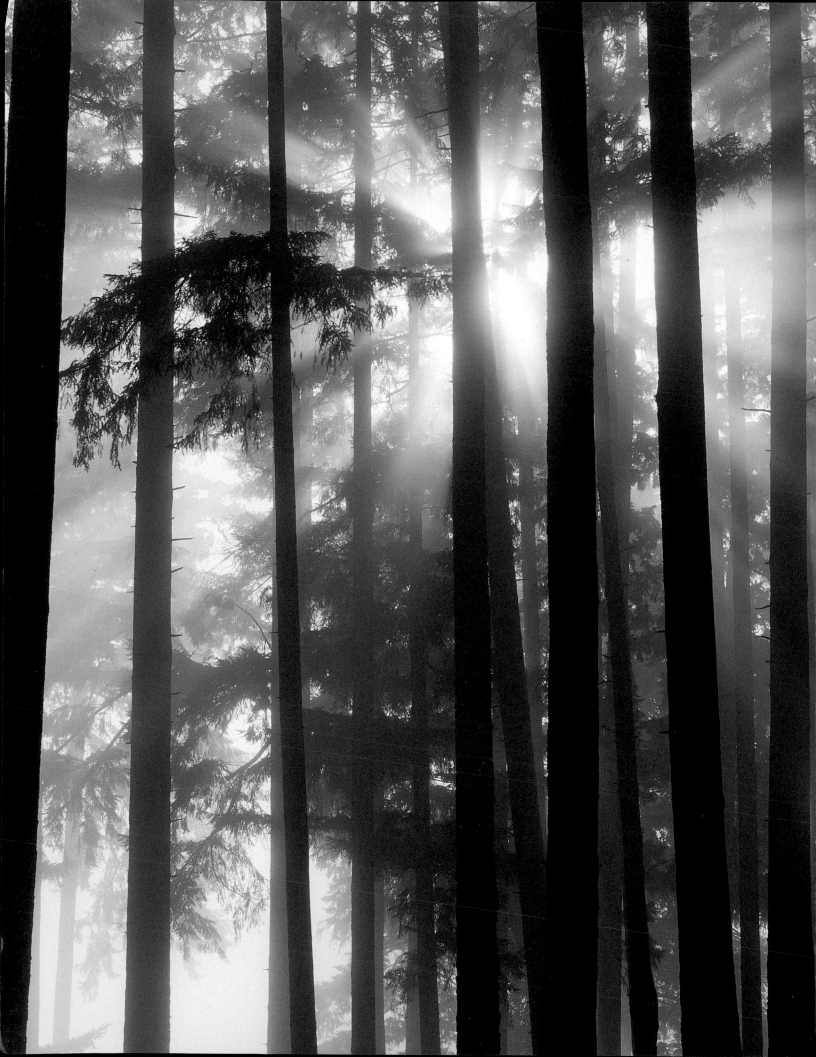

ANCIENT REALM OF THE PACIFIC NORTHWEST

Graham Osborne

TEXT BY
Wade Davis

FOREWORD BY DAVID SUZUKI

GREYSTONE BOOKS
VANCOUVER/TORONTO

CHELSEA GREEN PUBLISHING COMPANY
WHITE RIVER JUNCTION, VERMONT
TOTNES, ENGLAND

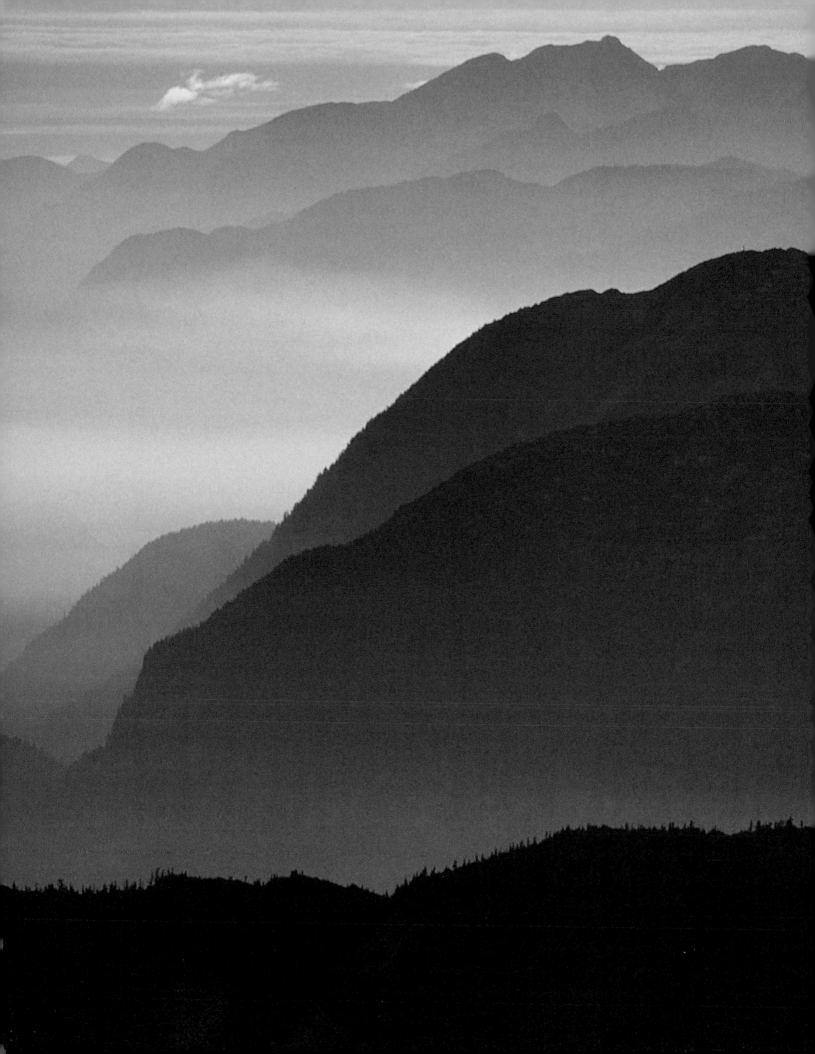

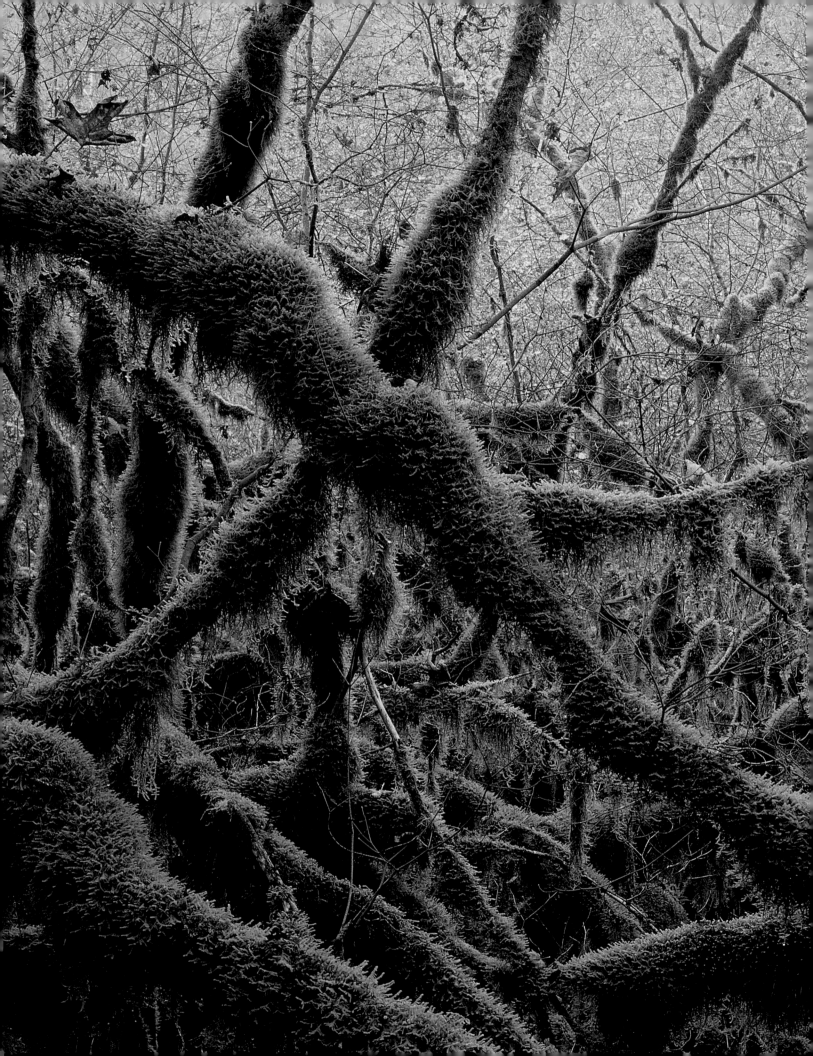

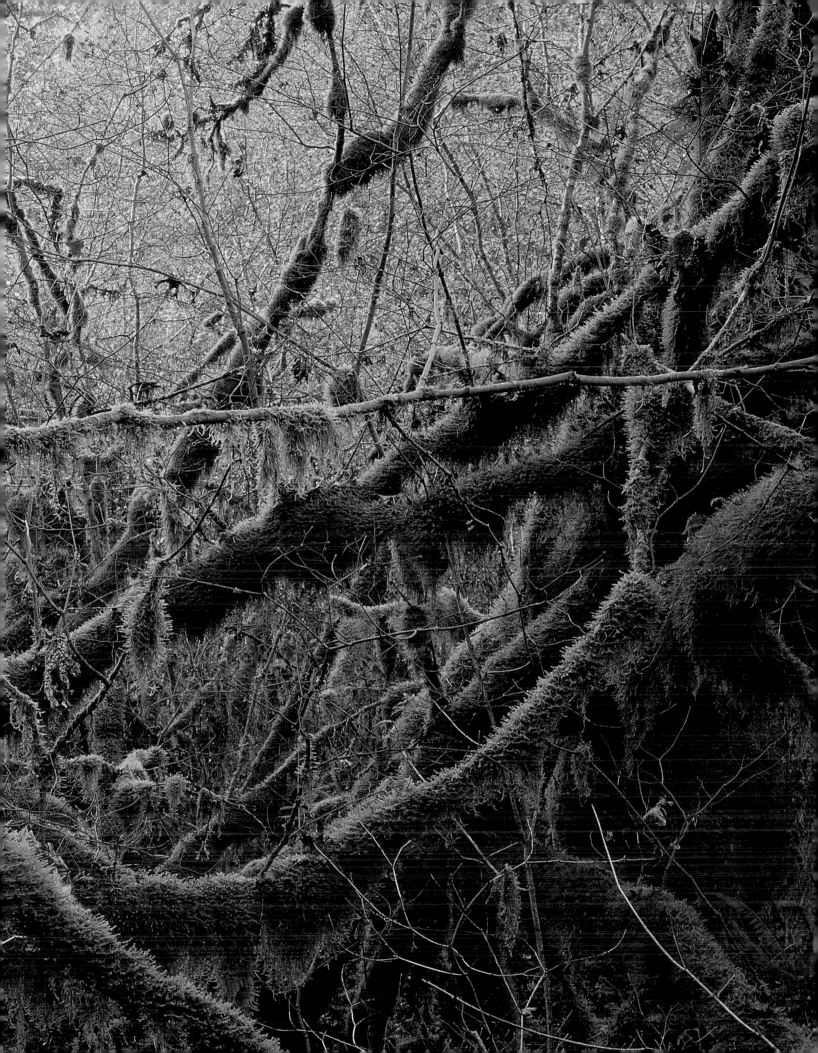

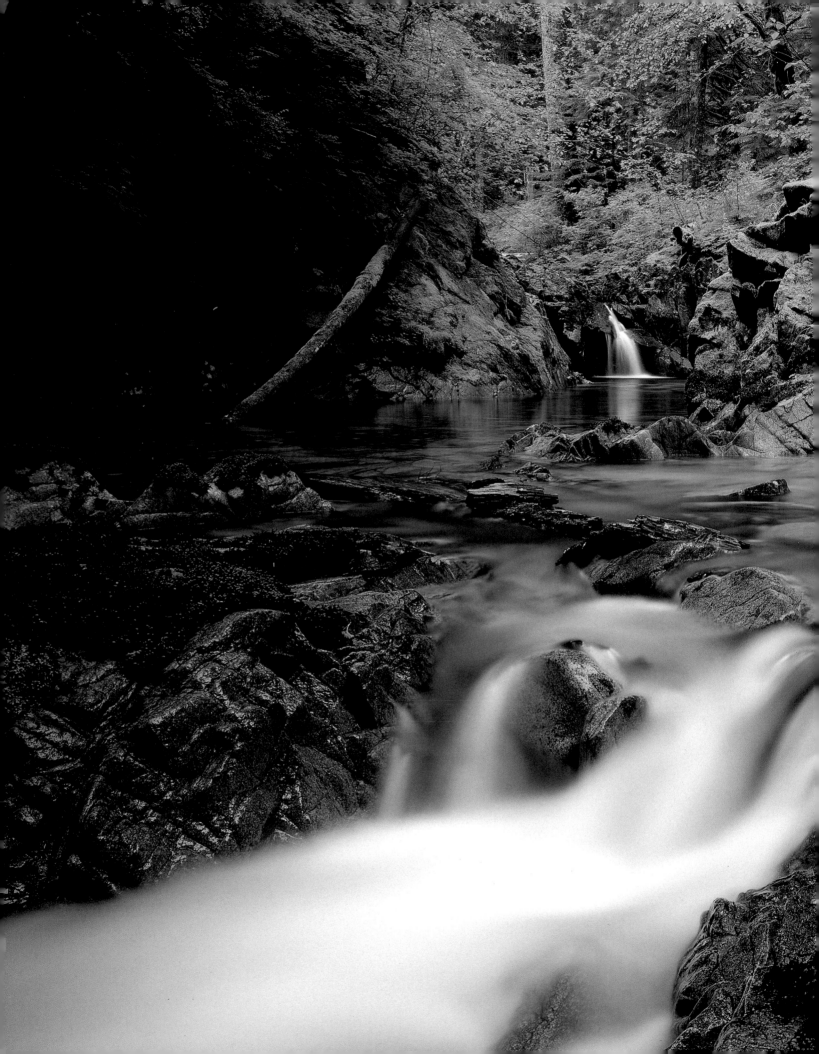

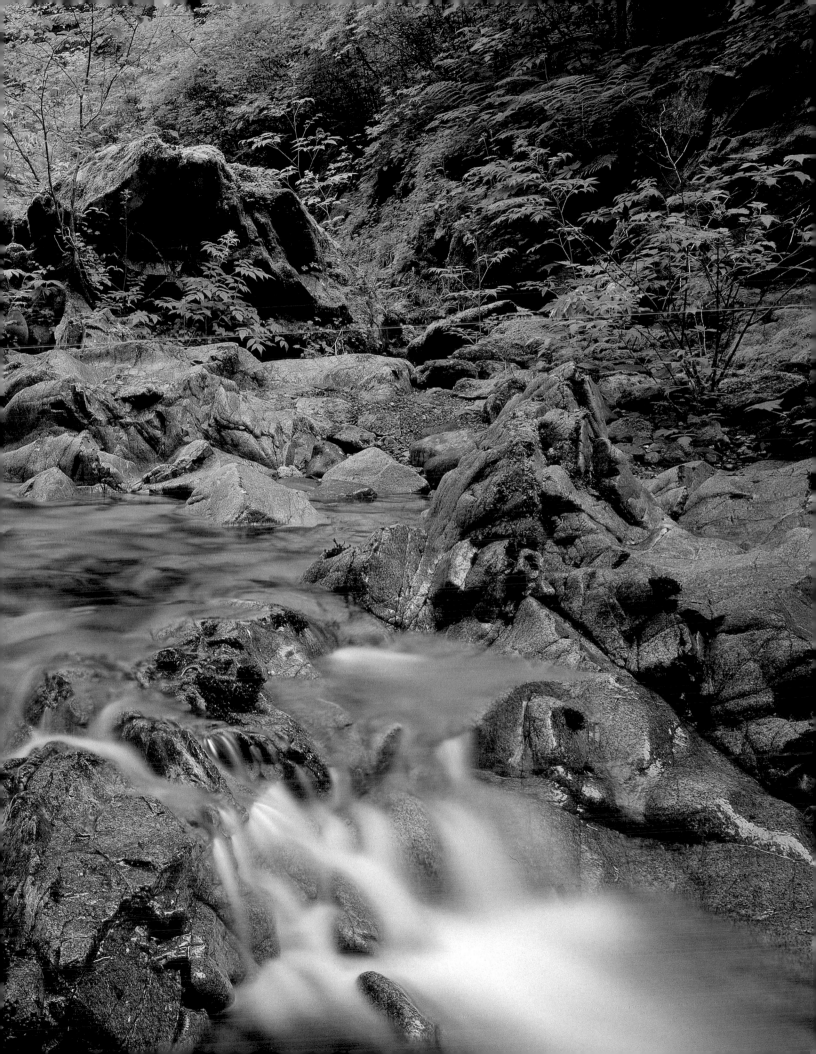

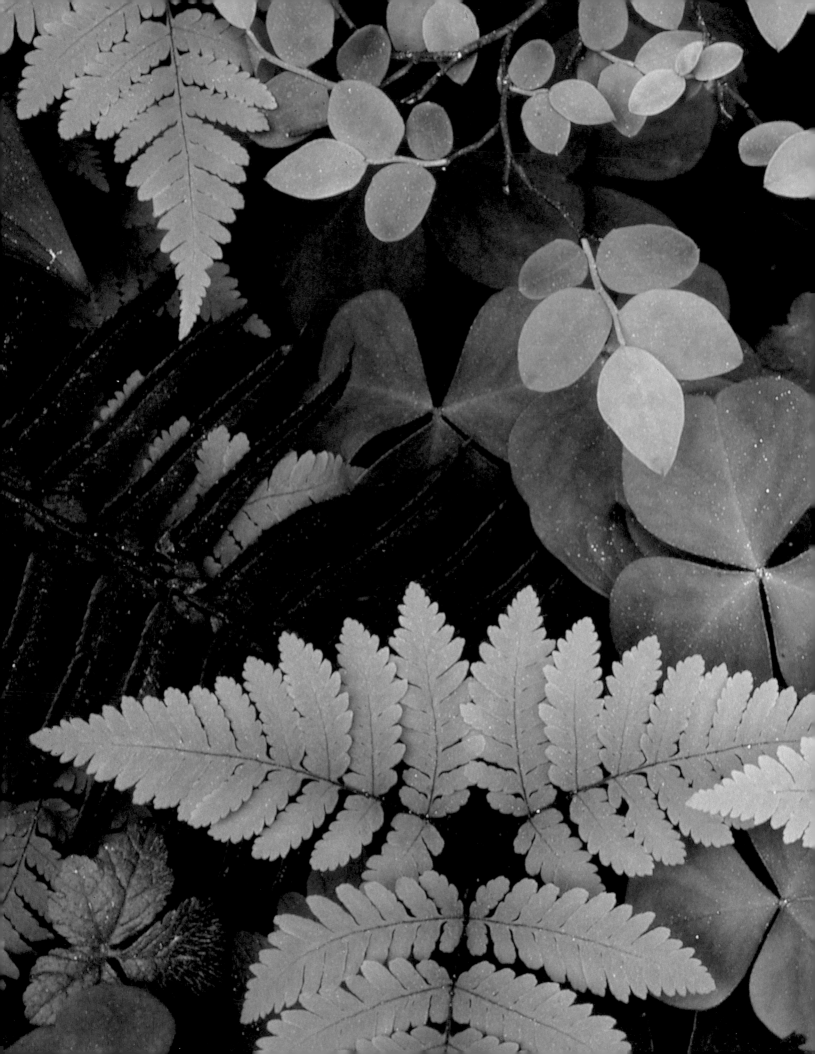

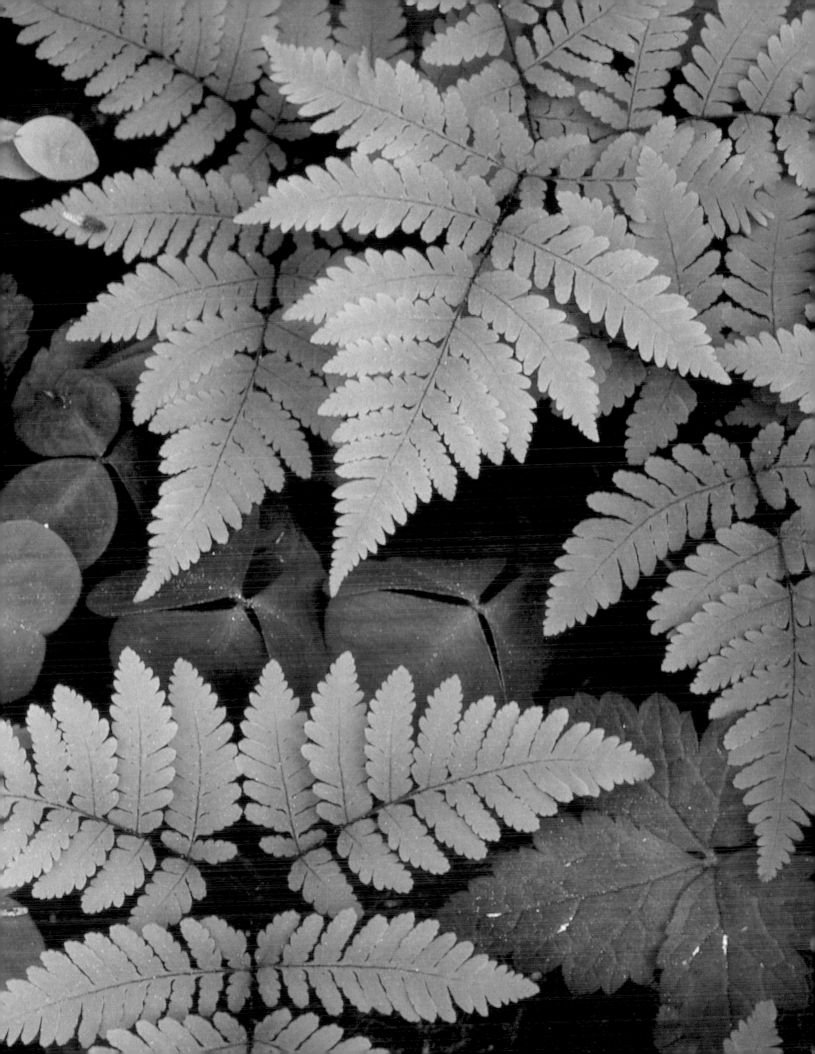

*I thank God for my parents, Rose and Ken Osborne, and
my grandma, Rozalia Garbiar, and for the gift of these great forests
I have been so privileged to photograph.* —G.O.

No old-growth fibre has been used in the paper for this book.

Page 2: Sunrise, Nahatlatch Valley, British Columbia

Pages 4—5: Last light near Cape Caution, midcoast of British Columbia

*Pages 6—7: Old growth along the west bank of the Squamish River,
British Columbia*

Pages 8—9: Vine maples, Elwha Valley, Washington

*Pages 10—11: Upper Carmanah Creek, Carmanah Pacific Provincial
Park, British Columbia*

Pages 12—13: Ferns and oxalis, Queets River, Washington

*Right: An unnamed waterfall along Ellerslie Lake, midcoast of British
Columbia*

Photographs copyright © 1998 by Graham Osborne
Text copyright © 1998 by Wade Davis
First paperback edition, 2000

00 01 02 03 04 5 4 3 2 1

Greystone Books
A division of
Douglas & McIntyre Ltd.
2323 Quebec Street, Suite 201
Vancouver, B.C. V5T 4S7

Canadian Cataloguing in Publication Data

Osborne, Graham, 1962–
   Rainforest

   ISBN 1-55054-620-1 (cloth)   ISBN 1-55054-763-1 (pbk)

   1. Rain forests—Northwest Coast of North America—Pictorial works.   2.
Rain forests—Northwest Coast of North America. I. Title.
QH104.5.P32082 1998   577.34'09795   C98-910272-6

Originated by Greystone Books and published simultaneously in the United
States of America by:
Chelsea Green Publishing Co.
P.O. Box 428
White River Junction, VT
05001
www.chelseagreen.com

U.S. Library of Congress Cataloging-in-Publication data available upon request.

Cover and book design by George Vaitkunas
Printed and bound in Singapore by C.S. Graphics Pte. Ltd.

The publisher gratefully acknowledges the support of the Canada Council of
the Arts and of the British Columbia Ministry of Tourism, Small Business and
Culture. The publisher acknowledges the financial support of the Government
of Canada through the Book Publishing Industry Development Program
(BPDIP) for its publishing activities.

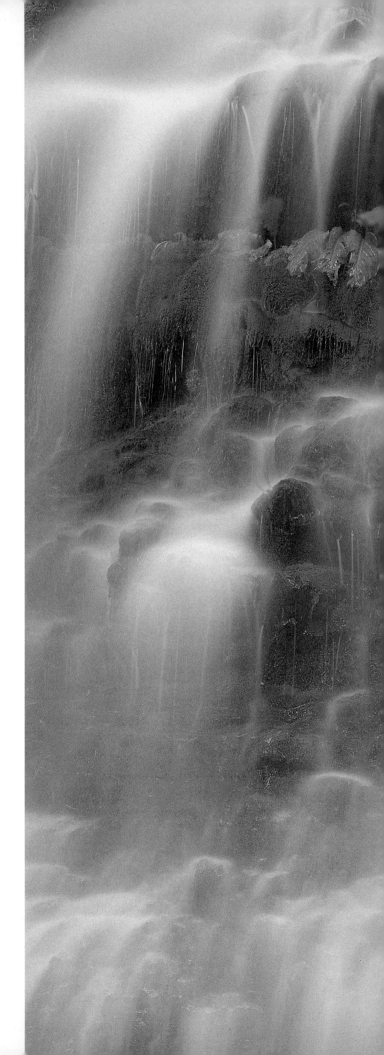

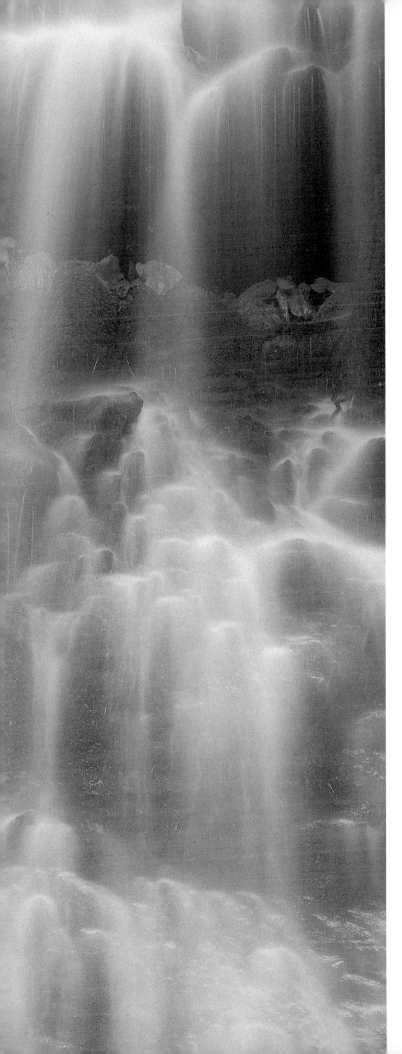

Contents

Foreword
by David Suzuki

As a species, we tend to value other species for their usefulness to us—how they can feed or clothe us, aid in scientific research or bring economic reward. In doing so, we overlook the exquisite interplay and unimaginable complexity of this tapestry on Earth that we call life. It is a perilous omission.

As an example, I spent my entire scientific career studying the genetics of *Drosophila melanogaster*, a fruit fly. My colleagues and I often referred to it half-jokingly as "a bag of chromosomes" because we bred these insects so that we could study the patterns of inheritance of their genes, not so that we could learn about the whole animal. Hundreds of geneticists have focussed on this one species and acquired profound insights into the intricate balance between the insect's genes and its development and behaviour. In the process, these geneticists have accumulated an impressive stable of mutants, including insects with twelve legs instead of six, embryos with two heads and no abdomen, and adults with wings growing from their eyes. At least eight Nobel Prizes have been earned by scientists working with *Drosophila*.

Impressive as these achievements are, there remain gaping holes in our understanding of the fruit fly's basic biology; for example, we have no idea how the insect survives the rigours of a Canadian winter. And *Drosophila melanogaster* is only one of thousands of species of fruit fly about which almost nothing is known. In our enchantment with the spectacular technical tools and intellectual insights of molecular biology, we have ignored the basic biology of the whole organism and its interaction with its surroundings.

In a similar way, we have looked at trees as commodities or resources to be assessed by their economic worth. As a result, we have become blind to the fact that they are part of a much larger whole. We make value judgements reflected in the way we talk—trees become "stems," "weeds" or "merchantable timber"; forests are "decadent" or "overmature," while an industrial plantation is a "normal forest." We make the mistaken assumption that trees planted in growth chambers or experimental plots are replicas of entire forests or ecosystems. I have been told that clearcut logging is part of "proper silvicultural practice" and that we know enough to be able to re-create the old-growth forests that are being torn down. But if we know so little about the fruit fly after billions of dollars and thousands of person-years have been spent researching this animal, how can anyone believe that we possess the knowledge to reproduce a forest?

The answer is that what the forest industry calls a forest is not a forest at all. It is simply an illusion that a grotesquely simplified collection of commercially useful trees planted like a field of tomatoes can be regarded as a forest. There is so much that we don't know about all the factors that comprise a forest—the soil, water, air, plants, soil microorganisms, insects and so on. Only nature and time have grown a forest in the fullest sense, and the forest industry's claims that it can grow high-quality trees as crops with "rotation cycles" of seventy or eighty years are either fantastic hallucinations or deliberate deceptions.

Every forest on the planet is unique. Perhaps the most important principle that molecular biology has taught us is that diversity, at the gene, species and ecosystem levels, is the source of resilience and adaptability as the environment changes over time. This living web of vast diversity is the very wellspring of the air, water and soil, which are constantly cleansed and replenished. Scientists are a long way from completing even a basic inventory of the biophysical components of the biosphere, let alone understanding how they interact to create such diverse ecosystems as rainforests, grasslands, estuaries and wetlands.

This eloquent book reminds us of the unfathomable beauty and complexity of our coastal forest while making us confront the crude musclepower of industrial forestry. Wade Davis's text presents powerful personal stories of the brute reality of logging and lets us think of the forest as a community of species, each exquisitely fitting into the whole, while Graham Osborne's images touch our emotions and spirit. Together, text and images appeal to both our hearts and our minds.

Photographer's Preface

I AWOKE AT 5:30 A.M. to the rattle of hard November rain. The temperature hovered a few degrees above freezing as I prepared my pack and gear for a long, wet day. Within twenty steps of the road the forest had swallowed me, a brisk baptism in the rain-soaked underbrush setting the tone for the rest of the hike. I worked the trailless bank of a small brook that gurgled down a steep little valley, sweating and slogging heavily uphill for almost 3 kilometres in the downpour. The creek was delightful. Pristine and clear, it tumbled pool by pool in a series of tiny fern-edged waterfalls through magnificent stands of barrel-chested cedars and nurse logs carpeted in seedlings and feather moss. Mist spirited through the canopy above, adding a certain primordial element. I felt I had stepped back in time, into an ancient forest exquisite in every element of its being. It was perhaps the most spectacular grove of old growth I had ever photographed.

For the next eight hours, the rainforest lived up to its billing, as a moist Pacific cold front pounded the coast. Soaking wet and chilled to the core, I worked feverishly to keep my equipment dry as I framed several compositions over the course of the day. The cool air, high humidity and wind-whipped rain repeatedly fogged my lens, threatening to put an end to the shoot. The conditions were miserable. But the images that unfolded before me were magical, and I felt privileged to be allowed an audience in such an Eden-like scene.

It was hard to leave the forest that afternoon. The day had been a great success, despite the inclement weather that had soaked thousands of dollars' worth of camera gear, which now lay spread out and drying on my truck floor. The road out was equally magnificent. Darkness had hidden the forest during my arrival, but now daylight revealed ancient big leaf maples, their massive limbs draped in delicate tapestries of moss, lichens and licorice ferns, many hanging 2 metres or more. Sitka spruce towered out of the valley bottom to cathedral heights, true monarchs of the rainforest. Most people would not experience a forest like this in their lifetimes, I thought, as I replayed the images of the day over in my mind.

Then, without warning, the forest changed radically. In contrast to the great stands I had encountered earlier, I was now driving through masses of stunted evergreens, crowded unnaturally together and competing for space. Through the maze of narrow trunks, I could see an occasional giant stump. Decayed and lifeless, these stumps stood in silent testimony to what had been. In the distance, I could see massive clearcuts scarring the mountainside for miles. Over two-thirds of this great valley had been levelled.

Signs along the road declared New Forest Planted, with an approximate date. I stopped at one of the older stands of "new forest" and walked in. It resembled dozens of other second-growth forests I had explored. The trees were emaciated and pathetic, so tightly packed that little light filtered through the dense canopy. The understorey was dark and lifeless, a tangle of branches. Where once diversity had ruled and thousands of species had shared space, now only a few hardy colonizers dominated. This forest held nothing in common with the forest I had just hiked, feeling strangely sterile in contrast. I wondered how such destruction could be justified. The ancestral forest that once reigned here was a world treasure, like no other place on earth. I wondered how many people really understood what had been lost. Had others seen this ancient forest the way I had?

PERHAPS ONE of the most insidious threats to our old-growth forests is the fact that they can be replanted. There is a great misconception that after a forest is logged it is simply resown and that in time this second growth, like a field of wheat, will return to its former state. A "tree farm"

in every sense. But in every sense—ecologically, economically, aesthetically—nothing could be further from the truth.

The biological impacts of logging are deeply traumatic, unalterably affecting a forest's ability to regenerate and heal itself. Few if any harvests of man render such widespread and irreversible damage on such a tremendous scale. There is an air of finality to a clearcut. A great primordial web of life has been torn up by its roots. The interrelationship of organisms built gradually over centuries could never be duplicated, even if the area were left fallow a millennium or more. Nutrient cycles have been fractured and depleted. The earth has been stripped— leached and sucked of its goodness. Ton upon ton of biomass has been permanently removed, the nurturing elements of the soil locked deep within the complex organic bonds of uncountable board feet. What remains could never raise a second forest even modestly equivalent to the first. All this we lose with unarguable permanence.

If it were possible, I would prefer never to see another wild tree cut. But most if not all people see an inherent unreasonableness to such a proposition. It seems that too much of what we all hold dear rests on the continued harvest of our forests in some form. But the gluttony of previous decades has come back to cast a deep shadow of uncertainty, both on our ancient forests and on the industry that was built on them. Past mismanagement coupled with increased mechanization and a dwindling resource now threatens a way of life, both in human and ecological terms. We are all responsible, either in large or small part, for allowing the development of such grave circumstances, and I cannot help but feel the deepest compassion for the families that are now experiencing the most profound effects of our shortsightedness.

As a resource, our forests may be seen as renewable to some degree. But as a biological treasure, part of God's creation entrusted to our stewardship, our ancient stands are irreplaceable. We must start to see the value in this thinking, as keepers of a natural heritage and answerable to world generations, both present and future. The misconception that our forests are endless and here solely for our harvesting must change.

In the six years I spent photographing for this book, the finite nature of our rainforests was repeatedly driven home to me. One need only fly over the clearcut-ravaged landscape of Vancouver Island to understand the fate that awaits the rest of our coastline. I used to take some comfort in the idea of a great wilderness reserve of old growth to the north, untouched by industry for the most part. But during several trips along the mid- and north coasts of British Columbia, I was stunned to discover watershed after watershed already harvested or high-graded. Most of the remaining valleys were well mapped out for future cutting over the next two or three decades. I had been lulled into a sense of complacency that has influenced most if not all of us to some extent, and this was a wake-up call.

And so began the efforts towards this book. I wanted to capture the complexity and richness of the rainforest, its lush beauty, the intimate connection between land, water, weather and life that makes these great forests unique in the world. I also wanted to convey a sense of the ancient ecosystem that is nurtured here and of how diverse and irreplaceable it is, focussing less on what has been lost and more on what is left. Sadly, well over half the locations presented on these pages will likely be logged.

It is my hope that this book will contribute to the prudent conservation of the last, tenuous remnants of our once great old-growth stands. Perhaps these images will help reawaken in each of us our role as earthly stewards and instill in us a true reverence and appreciation for these primordial forests we have been so abundantly blessed with.

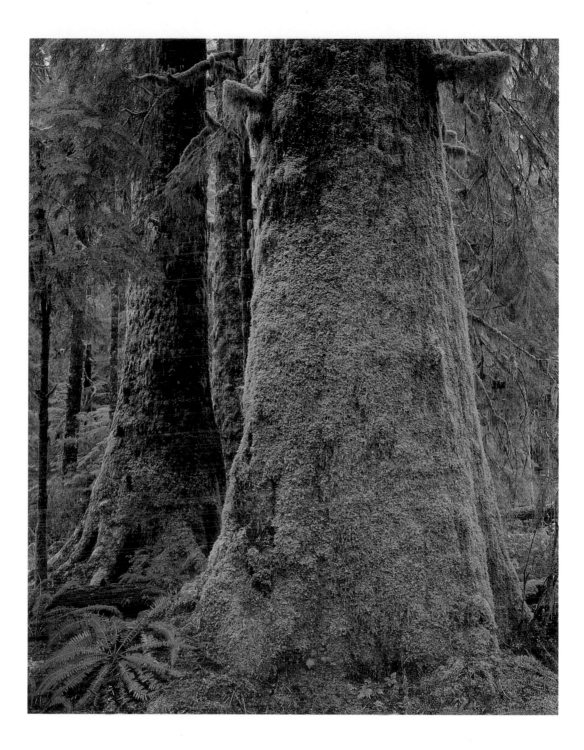

Giant Sitka spruce, Stoltmann
Stand in the Heaven Grove,
Carmanah Pacific Provincial
Park, British Columbia

Rainforest

IN THE SHADOW OF RED CEDAR, along a stream coloured by salmon, in a place where plants draw food from the air and small creatures living on dew never touch the forest floor, it is difficult to imagine a time when the coastal temperate rainforests of North America did not exist. Today these immense and mysterious forests, which in scale and wonder dwarf anything to be found in the tropics, extend in a vast arc from northern California 3000 kilometres north and west to the Copper River and the Gulf of Alaska. Home to myriad species of plants and animals, a constellation of life unique on earth, these forests spread between sea and mountain peak, reaching across and defying national boundaries as they envelop all who live within their influence in an unrivalled frontier of the spirit.

It is a world anchored in the south by giant sequoias, the most massive of living beings, and coast redwoods that soar above the fog banks of Mendocino. In the north two trees flourish, western hemlock, with its delicate foliage and finely furrowed bark, and Sitka spruce, most majestic of all, a stunningly beautiful species with blue-green needles that are salt tolerant and capable of extracting minerals and nutrients from sea spray. In between, along the silent reaches of the midcoast of British Columbia, behind a protective veil of Sitka spruce, grow enormous stands of Douglas fir. Intermingled with hemlock and fir, and found wherever the land is moist and the rains abundant, is perhaps the most important denizen of the Pacific slope, the western red cedar, the tree that made possible the florescence of the great and ancient cultures of the coast.

To walk through these forests in the depths of winter, when the rain turns to mist and settles softly on the moss, is to step back in time. Two hundred million years ago vast coniferous forests formed a mantle across the entire planet. Dinosaurs evolved long, supple necks to browse high among the branches of the trees. Then evolution took a great leap and the flowers were born. What made them unique was a mechanism of pollination and fertilization that changed the course of life on earth. In the more primitive conifers, the plant must produce the basic food for the seed with no certainty that it will be fertilized. In the flowering plants, by contrast, fertilization itself sparks the creation of the seed's food reserves. In other words, unlike the conifers, the flowering plants make no investment without the assurance that a viable seed will be produced. As a result of this and other evolutionary advances, the flowering plants came to dominate the earth in an astonishingly short period of time. Most conifers went extinct, and those that survived retreated to the margins of the world, where a small number of species managed to maintain a foothold by adapting to especially harsh conditions. Today, at a conservative estimate, there are over 250,000 species of flowering plants. The conifers have been reduced to a mere 700 species, and in the tropics, the hotbed of evolution, they have been almost completely displaced.

On all the earth, there is only one region of any size and significance where, because of unique climatic conditions, the conifers retain their former glory. Along the northwest coast of North America the summers are hot and dry, the winters cold and wet. Plants need water and light to create food. Here in the summer there is ample light for photosynthesis but not enough water for most deciduous trees, except in low-lying areas where broad-leafed species such as red alder, cottonwood and vine maple flourish. In the winter, when both water and light are sufficient, the low temperatures cause the flowering plants to lose their leaves and become dormant. The evergreen conifers, by contrast, are able to grow throughout the long winters, and since they use water more efficiently than broad-leafed plants, they also thrive during the dry summer months. The result is an ecosystem so rich and so productive that the biomass in the best sites is easily four times as great as that of any comparable area in the tropics.

Indeed, it is the scale and abundance of the coastal rainforests that overwhelms the visitor. White pine, the tallest tree of the eastern deciduous forests, barely reaches 60 metres; in the coastal rainforests there are thirteen species that grow higher, with the redwoods reaching nearly 120 metres, taller than a twenty-five-storey building. Red cedars can be 6 metres or more across at the base. The footprint of a Douglas fir would crush a small cabin. The trunk of a western hemlock, a miracle of biological engineering, stores thousands of litres of water and supports branches festooned with as many as 70 million needles, all capturing the light of the sun. Spread out on the ground, the needles of a single tree would create a photosynthetic surface ten times the size of a football field.

These giant trees delight, but the real wonder of the forest lies in the details, in the astonishingly complex relationships. A pileated woodpecker living in the hollow of a snag, tiny seabirds laying their eggs in underground nests among the roots of an ancient cedar, marbled murrelets nesting in a depression in the moss in the fork of a canopy tree, rufous hummingbirds returning each spring, their migrations timed to coincide with the flowering of salmonberries. In forest streams dwell frogs with tails and lungless salamanders that live by absorbing oxygen through the skin. Strange amphibians, they lay their eggs not in water but on land, in moist debris and fallen logs.

Invertebrate life is remarkably diverse. Within the crown of a single tree may be found as many as 1500 species. The first survey to systematically explore the forest canopy in the Carmanah Valley of Vancouver Island yielded 15,000 species, a third of the invertebrates known to exist in all of Canada. Among the survey's collections were 500 species previously unknown to science. Life is equally rich and abundant on the forest floor. Here are 12 species of slugs, slimy herbivores that in some areas comprise as much as 70 per cent of the animal biomass. A square metre of soil may support 2000 earthworms, 40,000 insects, 120,000 mites, 120 million nematodes and millions upon millions of protozoa and bacteria, all alive, moving through the earth, feeding, digesting, reproducing and dying.

None of these creatures, of course, live in isolation. In nature, no event stands alone. Every biological process, each chemical reaction, leads to the unfolding of other possibilities for life. Tracking these strands through an ecosystem is as complex as untangling the distant threads of memory from a myth. For years, even as industrial logging created clearcuts the size of small nations, the coastal rainforests were among the least studied ecosystems on the planet. Only within the last decade or two have biologists begun to understand and chart the dynamic forces and complex ecological relationships that allow these magnificent forests to exist.

One begins with wind and rain, the open expanse of the Pacific and the steep escarpment of mountains that makes possible the constant cycling of water between land and sea. Autumn rains last until those of spring, and months pass without a sign of the sun. Sometimes the rain falls as mist, and moisture is raked from the air by the canopy of the forest. At other times, the storms are torrential and daily precipitation is measured in centimetres. The rains draw nutrients from the soil, carrying vital food into rivers and streams that fall away to the sea and support the greatest coastal marine diversity on earth. In the estuaries and tidal flats of British Columbia, in shallows that merge with the wetlands, are found six hundred types of seaweed, seventy species of sea stars. Farther offshore vast underwater kelp forests shelter hundreds of forms of life, which in turn support a food chain that reaches into the sky to nourish dozens of species of seabirds.

The land provides for life in the sea, but the sea in turn nurtures the land. Birds deposit excrement in the moss, yielding tonnes of nitrogen and phosphorus that are washed into the soil by winter rains. Salmon return by the millions to their native streams, providing food for eagles and ravens, grizzly and black bears, killer whales, river otters and more than twenty other mammals of the sea and forest. Their journey complete, the sockeye and coho, chinooks, chums and pinks drift downstream in death and are slowly absorbed back into the nutrient cycle of life. In the end there is no separation between forest and ocean, between the creatures of the land and those of the sea. Every living thing on the rain coast ultimately responds to the same ecological rhythm. All are interdependent.

The plants that dwell on land nevertheless face unique challenges, especially that of securing nutrients from thin soils leached by rain throughout much of the year. The tangle of ecological adaptations that has evolved in response is nothing short of miraculous. As much as a fifth of the biomass in the foliage of an old-growth Douglas fir, for example, is an epiphytic lichen, *Lobaria oregana*, which fixes nitrogen directly from the air and passes it into the ecosystem. The needles of Sitka spruce absorb phosphorus, calcium and magnesium, and their high rate of transpiration releases moisture to the canopy, allowing the lichens to flourish.

On the forest floor thick mats of sphagnum and other mosses filter rainwater and protect the mycelial mats of hundreds of species of fungi; these elements form one of the richest mushroom floras on earth. Mycelia are the vegetative phase of a fungus, small hairlike filaments that spread through the organic layer at the surface of the soil, absorbing food and precipitating decay. A mushroom is simply the fruiting structure, the reproductive body. As the mycelia grow, they constantly encounter tree roots. If the species combination is the right one, chemical signals spark and a remarkable biological event unfolds. Fungus and tree come together to form mycorrhizae, a symbiotic partnership that allows both to benefit. The tree provides the fungus with sugars created from sunlight. The mycelia in turn enhance the tree's ability to absorb nutrients and water from the soil. They also produce growth-regulating chemicals that promote the production of new roots and enhance the immune system. Without this union, no tree could thrive. Western hemlocks are so dependent on mycorrhizal fungi that their roots barely pierce the surface of the earth, even as their trunks soar into the canopy.

The story only gets better. All life requires nitrogen for the creation of proteins. Nitrates, a basic source, are virtually absent from the acidic, heavily leached soils of the rainforest. The mycorrhizae, however, contain not only nitrogen-fixing bacteria that produce this vital raw material but also a yeast culture that promotes the growth of both the bacteria and the fungus. There are scores of different mycorrhizae—the roots of a single Douglas fir may have as many as forty types—and like any form of life, the fungus must compete, reproduce and find a means to disperse its spore. The fruiting body in many cases is an underground mushroom or a truffle. When mature, it emits a pungent odour that seeps through the soil to attract rodents, flying squirrels and red-backed voles, delicate creatures that live exclusively on a refined diet of truffles. As the voles move about the forest, they scatter droppings, neat little bundles of feces that contain yeast culture, fungal spores and nitrogen-fixing bacteria—in short, all that is required to inoculate roots and prompt the creation of new mycorrhizae.

Fungi bring life to the forest both by their ability to draw nutrients to the living and by their capacity to transform the dead. In old-growth forests 20 per cent of the biomass—as much as 600 tonnes per hectare—is retained in fallen debris and snags. There is as much nutrition on the ground as there is within it. The moss on the forest floor is so dense that virtually all seedlings sprout from the surface of rotting wood, stumps and logs, which may take several hundred years to decay.

When a tree falls in the forest, it is immediately attacked by fungi and a multitude of insects. The wood provides a solid diet of carbohydrates. To secure proteins and other nutrients, the fungi deploy natural antibiotics to kill nitrogen-fixing bacteria. Chemical attractants emitted by the fungi draw in other prey, such as nematode worms, which are dispatched with exploding poison sacs and an astonishing arsenal of microscopic weapons. The assault on the log comes from many quarters. Certain insects, incapable of digesting wood directly, exploit fungi to do the work. Ambrosia beetles, for example, deposit fungal spores in tunnels bored into the wood. After the spores germinate, the tiny insects cultivate the mushrooms on miniature farms that flourish in the dark.

In time other creatures appear—mites and termites, carpenter ants that chew long galleries in the wood and establish captive colonies of aphids that produce honeydew from the sap of plants. Eventually, as the log progresses through various stages of decay, other scavengers join the fray, including those that consume white cellulose, turning wood blood-red and reducing the heartwood to dust. An inch of soil may take a thousand years to accumulate. Organic debris may persist for centuries. Dead trees are the life of the forest, but their potential is realized only slowly and with great patience.

This observation leads to perhaps the most extraordinary mystery of all. Lush and astonishingly prolific, the coastal temperate rainforests are richer in their capacity to produce the raw material of life than any other terrestrial ecosystem on earth. The generation of this immense natural wealth is made possible by a vast array of biological interactions so complex and sophisticated as to suggest an evolutionary lineage drifting back to the dawn of time. Yet all evidence indicates that these forests emerged only within the last few thousand years. In aspect and species composition they may invoke the great coniferous forests of the distant geologic past, but as a discrete and evolving ecosystem the coastal temperate rainforests are still wet with the innocence of birth.

In the beginning what is today British Columbia was a place of turmoil and ice. A glacial sheet more than 1800 metres deep covered the Interior, forging mountains and grinding away valleys as it moved over the land, determining for all time the fate of rivers. On the coast giant tongues of ice carved deep fjords beneath the sea. The sea level fell by 90 metres, and the sheer weight of ice depressed the shoreline to some 230 metres below its current level. A mere fourteen thousand years ago, an instant in geologic time, the ice began to melt and the glaciers retreated for the last time. The ocean invaded the shore, inundating coastal valleys and islands. But the land, freed at last of the weight of eons, literally sprang up. Within a mere thousand years the water drained back into the sea, and the coastline became established more or less in the place it is today.

It was only in the wake of these staggering geological events that the forests came into being. At first the land was dry and cold, an open landscape of aspen and lodgepole pine. Around ten thousand years ago, even as the first humans appeared on the coast, the air became more moist and Douglas fir slowly began to displace the pine. Sitka spruce flourished, though hemlock and red cedar remained rare. Gradually the climate became warmer, with long seasons without frost. As more and more rain fell, endless banks of grey clouds sheltered the trees from the radiant sun. Western hemlock and red cedar expanded their hold on the south coast, working their way north at the expense of both fir and Sitka spruce.

For the first people of the rain coast this ecological transition became an image from the dawn of time, a memory of an era when Raven slipped from the shadow of cedar to steal sunlight and cast the moon and stars into the heavens. Mythology enshrined natural history, for it was the diffusion of red cedar that allowed the great cultures of the Pacific Northwest to emerge. The nomadic hunters and gatherers who for centuries had drifted with the seas along the western shores of North America were highly adaptive, taking advantage of every new opportunity for life. Although humans had inhabited the coast for at least five thousand years, specialized tools first appear in the archaeological record around 3000 B.C., roughly the period when red cedar came into its present dominance in the forests. A highly distinctive art form developed by 500 B.C. Over the next millennium a dramatic shift in technology and culture occurred. Large cedar structures were in use a thousand years before the Christian era. Stone mauls and wooden wedges, obsidian blades and shells honed to a razor's edge allowed the highly durable wood to be worked into an astonishing array of objects, which in turn expanded the potential of the environment.

Although in time some five hundred plants would be used on the coast, red cedar was from the beginning the tree of life. Its soft and pliant inner bark provided cordage and the fibre that was woven into clothing. Steamed, the wood could be bent into boxes that allowed for the efficient storage of food, especially salmon, berries and eulachon oil. Cedar provided armour and weapons for war, hewn planks for housing and dugout canoes for transportation, fishing and hunting whales and seals. It also provided the template upon which dreams could be brought

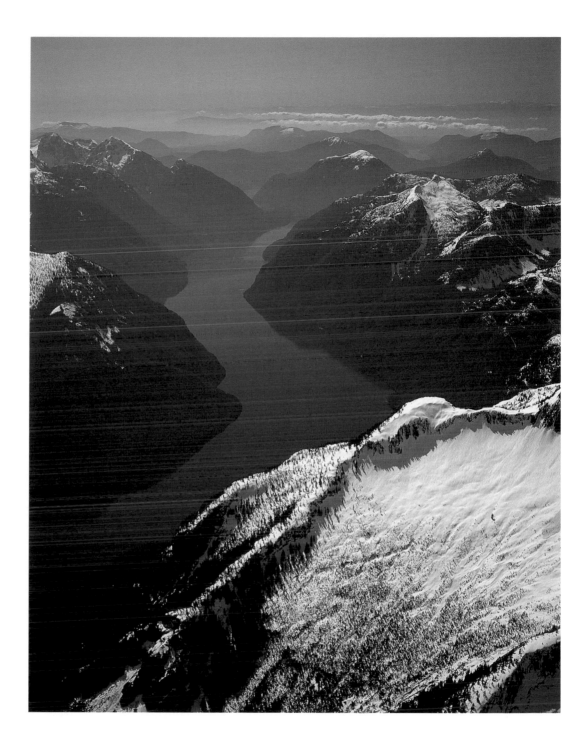

A fjord near Desolation Sound,
British Columbia

into daylight, families celebrated and mythological time remembered in the form of crests, memories of the dead displayed for generations of the living.

With cedar as the material foundation of culture, and salmon and other marine resources providing the mainstay of the diet, the seafarers forged the most complex civilization ever to emerge without benefit of agriculture. Although living in permanent settlements, in a stratified world of commoners, slaves, shamans and princely elite, the people remained foragers, nomads of the open seas, hunters whose lives depended on their relationship with the wild. Unlike so many who had succumbed to the cult of the seed, the nations of the coast believed in the power of animals, accepted the existence of magic, acknowledged the potency of the spirit. The physical world presented but one face of reality. Behind it existed an inner world of meaning, a place reached through transformation, a passage familiar to shamans and recalled by everyone during the great winter dances and ritual celebrations.

Living from nature, and lacking the technology to dominate it, the people watched the earth for signs. The flight of eagles helped fishermen track salmon. Sandhill cranes heralded the onset of herring runs. The flowering of certain plants brought families to the shore to gather clams, but if ravens and crows abandoned the beach, so did the people, for it was a sure indication that the shellfish were toxic. Between humans and animals there was a constant dialogue, expressed in physical action, in gesture and repartee, but also in myths and stories that resonated with magical and mystical ideas. The Tlinglit addressed plants as spirits, offering prayers before harvesting a tree. Nuu-chah-nulth ceremonies sought protection for the hunter and beseeched whales to give freely of their lives. When raging currents threatened Haida war parties, the paddlers scattered swan feathers upon the water to calm the sea.

Encounters with grizzly bears brought power to the Gitksan. The Kwagiulth dispatched initiates into the forest to seek Huxwhukw and the Crooked Beak of Heaven, cannibal spirits living at the north end of the world.

Though neither sentimental nor weakened by nostalgia, these indigenous cultures forged through time and ritual a traditional mystique of the earth that was based not only on deep attachment to the land but also on far more subtle intuition—the idea that the land was breathed into being by human consciousness. Mountains, rivers and forests were not perceived as inanimate, as mere props on a stage upon which the human drama unfolds. For these societies, the land was alive, a dynamic force to be embraced and transformed by the human imagination. Whether this was true in some absolute sense is not the point. Rather the significance lies in the manner in which the conviction played out in the day-to-day lives of the people. A child raised to revere the forest as the domain of the spirits will be a fundamentally different person from a child brought up to believe that a forest exists to be cut.

I WAS FIFTEEN when I first learned that all of these ancient forests, from California to Alaska, were dying. This startling information was presented to my biology class in a documentary film sponsored by Weyerhaeuser and featuring as host and narrator the actor Eddie Albert, famous for his role as the husband of Eva Gabor in the television hit *Green Acres*. It was difficult news to swallow. The script called for Mr. Albert to make his pronouncement while walking along a trail in a verdant grove of hemlocks and cedars. The trees were massive, 3 metres or more across at the base, and all were draped in lichens, which fused with the dense and lush moss of the forest floor. Mist hung in the air. From fallen logs sprouted wisps of red huckleberry and salal. A stream ran through the frame, and on either bank grew dense thickets of sword ferns and salmonberry.

"True, it looks healthy," Albert cautioned, " but don't let it fool you. This forest is dying."

Our teacher, a flaccid individual with a brilliant shock of red hair, explained the scientific foundation for Albert's astonishing assertion. Science had shown that the annual increment of cellulose in a young tree plantation was greater than that of an ancient forest. The old growth was, by definition, a forest in decline. The trees were over-mature. To see evidence of decadence, one had only to look at the deadfall, tonnes of rotting timber wasted on the forest floor. The goal of proper management was to replace these inefficient stands with fresh and productive new forests. A regime of carefully monitored clearcut logging would eliminate the old growth, the debris would be burned and the land sown with a uniform plantation composed of only the most up-to-date conifer seedlings. In short, modern forestry would clean up the mess inherited from nature.

Even as a teenager, sitting in a classroom overlooking the forested slopes of Vancouver Island, I had the sense that somebody was playing with a short deck. Industrial logging on a massive scale had been under way in British Columbia since the end of the Second World War. The rotation cycle—the rate at which forests were to be cut across the province, and thus the foundation of sustained yield forestry—was based on the assumption that all of the old growth would be cut and replaced with tree farms. The intrinsic value of the ancient forests had no place in the calculus of forest planning. The science of forestry provided the rationale for eradication. The obvious beneficiaries of such ideas and policies were the large timber concerns, including the sponsor of the film we had been obliged to watch.

Some years later, soon after graduating from university, I experienced firsthand the actual practice of modern forestry. Working for one of the largest timber companies in British Columbia, I spent a long winter in a logging camp near the west coast of Haida Gwaii, or the Queen Charlottes, as the islands were then commonly known. Hired as a forestry engineer, I worked as a surveyor, which meant that I spent most of my time in the primary forest, far ahead of the fallers and loggers, laying out roads and falling boundaries, determining the pattern in which the trees would come down. In the depth of winter our small crew moved through stands of red cedar, hemlock and Sitka spruce, trees as tall as cathedrals.

Inevitably there was, at least for me, an almost surreal quality to life in our remote camp, where men lived away from their families and made a living cutting down in minutes trees that had taken centuries to grow. The constant grinding of machinery, the disintegration of the forest into burnt slash and mud, the wind and sleet that froze on the rigging and whipped across the frozen bay etched patterns into the lives of the men. Still, no one in our camp had any illusions about what we were doing. All talk of sustained yield and overmature timber, decadent and normal forests, we left to government bureaucrats and company foresters. We used to laugh at the little yellow signs stuck on the sides of roads that only we would ever travel, announcing that 8 hectares had been replanted, as if it mattered in a clearcut that stretched to the horizon.

With haunting regularity, winter gales swept through the islands, and along the face of the forest exposed by the clearcut it was not unusual to encounter hectares of timber brought down by the wind. The result was a nightmare of overlapping trunks and roots, thousands of tonnes of wood weighted down with immense pressure and ready to explode with the first cut of a saw. Salvaging blowdown was dreaded work, dangerous and sometimes deadly. To mitigate the hazard and avoid the loss of fibre, government foresters permitted us to expand our cutblocks with the hope of establishing wind-firm boundaries. As a result, openings grew to encompass entire valleys, with the edge of the clearcut reaching to the ridge line of distant mountains. If a slope was deemed too steep to be logged, it was only because machinery could not get to it. Trees left standing by the edge of lakes or along streams inevitably blew over in the next storm. So these too were cut. My immediate boss used to joke about getting rid of the forest so that we could see something. Once, when he was questioned about the wisdom of logging across a salmon stream, he replied, "Hell, that's no creek, just a draw with a little bit of water in it."

Everyone knew, of course, that the ancient forests would never come back, at least not in any meaningful time frame. The tangle of half-hearted trees that grew up in the slash no more resembled the forest they had displaced than a wheat field resembles a wild prairie meadow. But nobody was worried about what we were doing. It was work, and living on the edge of that immense forest, people simply believed that it would go on forever.

If anyone in the government had a broader perspective, we never heard about it. Our camp was 30 kilometres by water across an inlet from a back road that ran 64 kilometres to the nearest forestry office. The government had cut back on overtime pay, and what with the statutory coffee and lunch breaks, the forestry employees had no way of travelling to our camp and back in less than 7½ hours. So they rarely came. The bureaucracy within the company was not much better. The mills down south often complained that our camp was sending them inferior grades of Douglas fir, which was surprising since the species does not grow on the islands of Haida Gwaii.

There were, of course, vague murmurs of ecological concern that filtered through to our camp. One morning in the cookhouse I ran into a friend of mine, a rock blaster named Archie, whose voice had been dusted by a lifetime of cigarettes and the dirt from a dozen mine explosions. He was reading an old newspaper, and the headline said something about Greenpeace.

"Sons of bitches don't know a damn thing about pollution," Archie said. He then proceeded to tell me about working conditions in the hard rock uranium mines of the Northwest Territories shortly after the Second World War. Concerned about the impact of radioactivity, the companies used to put the workers, including Archie, into large sealed chambers and release a gas with suspended particles of aluminum in it. The idea was that the aluminum would coat the lungs, and at the end of the shift the men would gag it up, together with any radioactive dust.

"Now that," growled Archie, "was environmental pollution."

In truth, it is difficult to know how much life in the midst of such destruction affected the men working in the forest. Some clearly believed blindly in the process and were hardened by that faith. Others were so transient, moving from camp to camp, sometimes on a monthly basis, that they never registered the full impact of any one logging show. Some just didn't care. Because the entire industry was so itinerant, no one ever developed a sense of belonging to a place. There was no attachment to the land, nor could there be, given what we were doing. In the slash of the clearcut, there was little room for sentiment.

Talk for the most part was of wages and survival. Logging is among the most perilous of occupations. Were a government office of five hundred employees to suffer the injury rate typical of a west coast logging camp, the office workers would see someone carried out on a stretcher virtually every day. Six or seven times a year there would be a death. In the year I worked in the woods I heard of a faller killed by a snag that pierced his hard hat and exited his groin. Another returned to camp a pile of wood chips and tattered flesh; his saw had kicked back and ripped a trench in his face. In a neighbouring camp, a trigger-happy rigging slinger blew in the main line before the chokermen were clear of the bight. The logs hung up, nose-dived into the ground and then, torn by the force of the yarder's two thousand horsepower, swung about like a giant scythe. One man was crushed beneath a hundred tonnes of spruce. Another miraculously escaped unscathed, losing only his hard hat. The third and youngest was struck in the back of the head. No one was able to find his face.

The fallers were a breed apart, the elite of the camp, rough-cut individuals willing to risk their lives in exchange for the highest industrial wages in the province. They loved the solitude of the forest, even when its silence was broken by the whine of their saws. In their massive hands these formidable machines could appear almost toylike. But each weighed 30 pounds, packed the power of an outboard motor and at full throttle drove 100 feet of sharpened steel chain around a 4-foot bar every second. Such a tool cuts through a 3-foot log in a minute, a leg in the wink of an eye. In time the vibration affects the circulation in the hands. Several old fallers in camp could only get to sleep at night by tying their hands above their heads to reduce the pain. Others dreamt of trees that twisted and split as they fell, or hollow snags that collapsed and exploded. One spoke of a friend who never returned from a shift. Buried by blowdown, his body was not found until the setting was logged.

It was impossible not to admire these men, but it was equally impossible to ignore the consequences of what we were doing. Week by week, month by month, the edge of the clearcut spread, consuming the forest and leaving in its wake a torn and desolate landscape, pounded by winter rains that carried away the thin soil in dark torrents to the sea. What ultimately happened to the land was irrelevant. It was simply abandoned to nature. In the nine months I spent in the camp I never saw a tree planted, let alone evidence of a sustained program of modern silviculture. I cannot recall a single decision that was influenced in any way by an ecological concern. The priority and focus of every aspect of the logging operation was the extraction of timber. Roads were built as cheaply and efficiently as possible and, with the exception of main-line corridors, expected to last only long enough to access the wood. Streams clogged by riprap, mountain sides etched with erosion and scarred by landslides, clearcuts piled high with wood, wasted and abandoned—these were the norm, the inevitable result not just of an economic imperative but of a way of thinking that viewed the forest as a resource to be exploited. As surely as a miner rips coal from the earth, we were cutting away the rainforest. It was a one-time deal, and everyone knew it.

Like all the others in camp, I was there to make money. On weekends, when our survey crew was down, I picked up overtime pay by working in the slash as a chokerman, wrapping the cables around the fallen logs so that the yarders could drag them to the landings where they were loaded onto the trucks. Setting beads was the most miserable job in a logging show, the bottom rung of the camp hierarchy.

One Saturday I was working in a setting high up on the mountain that rose above the camp. It had been raining all day and the winds were blowing from the southeast, dragging clouds across the bay and up the slope, where they hung up in the tops of the giant hemlocks and cedars that rose above the clearcut. We were working the edge of the opening, but the landing was unusually close by. It took no time at all for the mainline to haul the logs in and for the haulback to fling the chokers back to us.

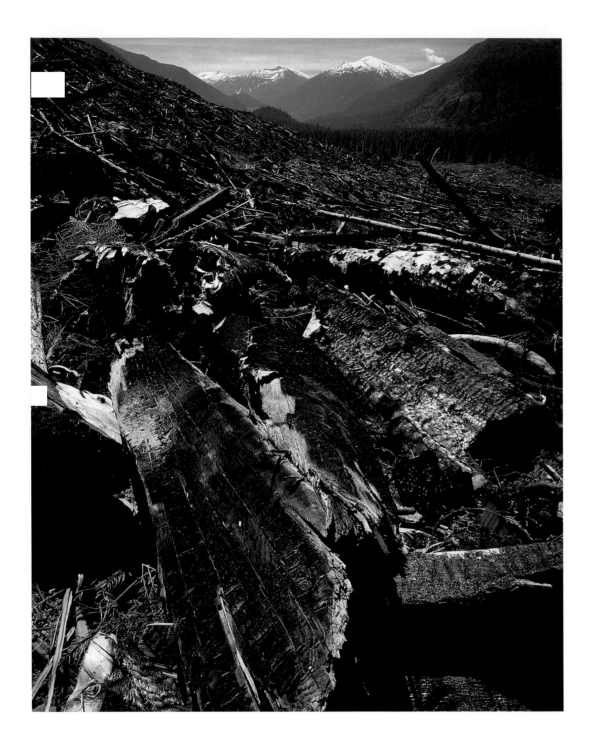

A clearcut in the upper Elaho Valley at the edge of the Stoltmann Wilderness, British Columbia

We had been highballing all day, and both my partner and I were a mess of mud, grease and tree sap. He was a Native youth, a Nisga'a from New Aiyansh on the Nass River, but that's all I knew about him.

Late in the afternoon something got fouled up on the landing and the yarder shut down. Suddenly it was quiet and you could hear the wind that had been driving sleet into our faces all day. My partner and I abandoned the slash for the shelter of the forest. We found a dry spot out of the wind in a hollow at the base of an enormous cedar and waited for the yarder to start up. We didn't speak. My partner kept staring off into the forest. All hunched up with the cold, we looked the same—orange hard hats, green-black rain gear, rubber corkboots. We shared a cigarette. I was watching his face as he smoked. It struck me as strange that here we were, huddled in the forest in silence, two young men from totally different worlds. I tried to imagine what it might have been like had we met but a century before, I perhaps a trader, he a shadow in the wet woods. His people had made a home in the forest for thousands of years. I thought of what this country must have been like when my own grandfather arrived. I saw in the forest around us a world that my own children might never know, that Nisga'a children would never know. I turned to my partner. The whistle blew on the landing.

"What the hell are we doing?" I asked.

"Working," he said. I watched him as he stepped back into the clearcut, and then I followed. We finished the shift and, in the falling darkness, rode to camp together in the back of the company crummy. That was the last I saw of him.

TWENTY YEARS HAVE PASSED since I left that camp, and much has changed in the forest industry. I've often wondered what became of that Nisga'a youth. It is a good bet that he is no longer working as a logger. Native workers rarely get promoted beyond the landing, and what's more, over the last two decades a third of all logging jobs have been lost. Industry blames environmentalists, but the truth lies elsewhere. All the conservation initiatives have not cost the unions more than a few hundred jobs, if that. In many sectors of the forest economy new regulations have in fact enhanced employment by mandating, for example, labour-intensive restorative efforts on cutover lands. Jobs have been sacrificed on a massive scale because industry in an intensely competitive global marketplace has consistently chosen efficiency and profit over employment.

In the last thirty years the volume of timber logged has increased threefold, but the number of jobs generated per unit of wood has been cut in half. Modern mills consume wood at twice the rate but use half the labour to produce the same volume. In many camps grapple yarders have eliminated rigging crews; two men now do the work of six. Automation together with dwindling timber supplies has put almost thirty thousand people out of work in British Columbia alone, and their jobs will not be replaced. Over fifty years ago exclusive timber rights to the most productive land in British Columbia were granted to private companies on the condition that they would provide employment to the people of the province. This social contract, the foundation of a tenure system that ultimately locked up 94 per cent of the commercially viable provincial forests in timber supply, has been broken and betrayed.

Still we keep cutting. In Oregon and Washington only 10 per cent of the original coastal rainforest remains. In California only 4 per cent of the redwoods have been set aside. In British Columbia roughly 60 per cent of the primary coastal forest has been logged, largely since 1950. In the two decades since I stood in the forest with that Nisga'a youth, over half of all timber ever extracted from the public forests of British Columbia has been taken.

*Coast Mountains at sunset,
near Wakeman Sound, British
Columbia*

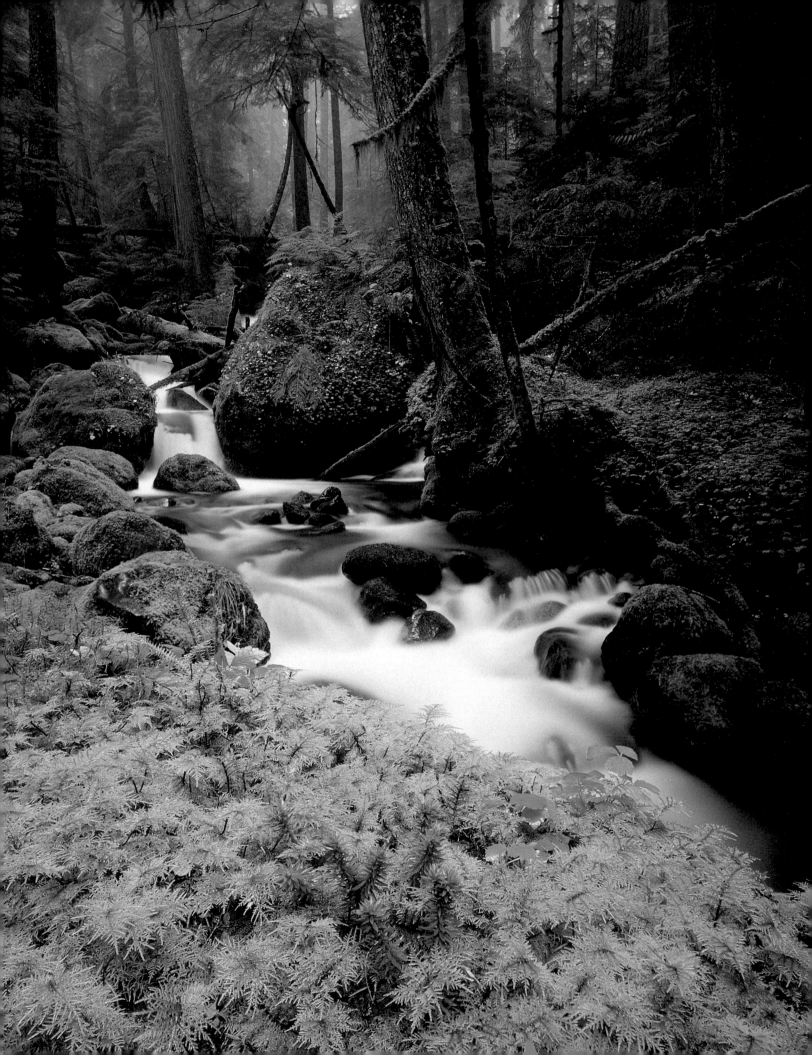

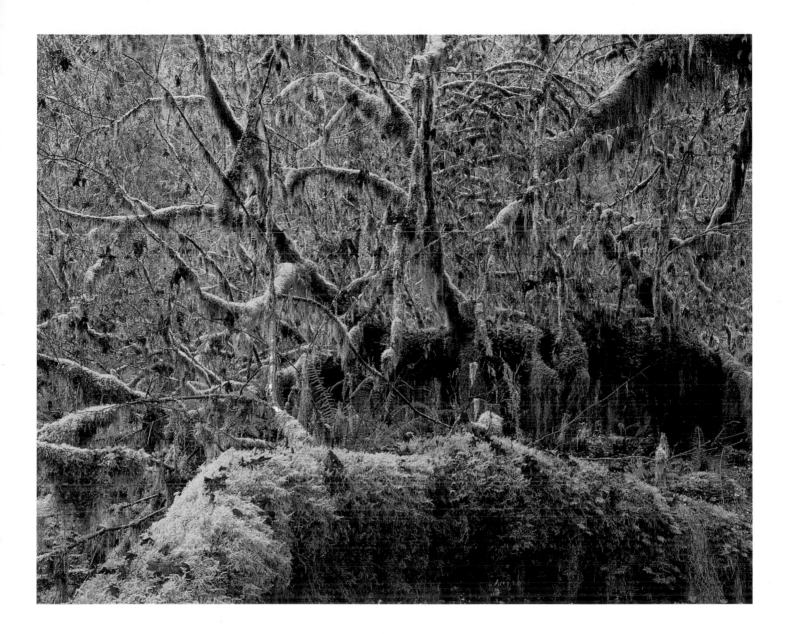

Facing page: Morse Creek
watershed, Olympic Peninsula,
Washington

Above: Hoh River Valley,
Olympic Peninsula, Washington

Overleaf: Old-growth stand near
Forks, Washington

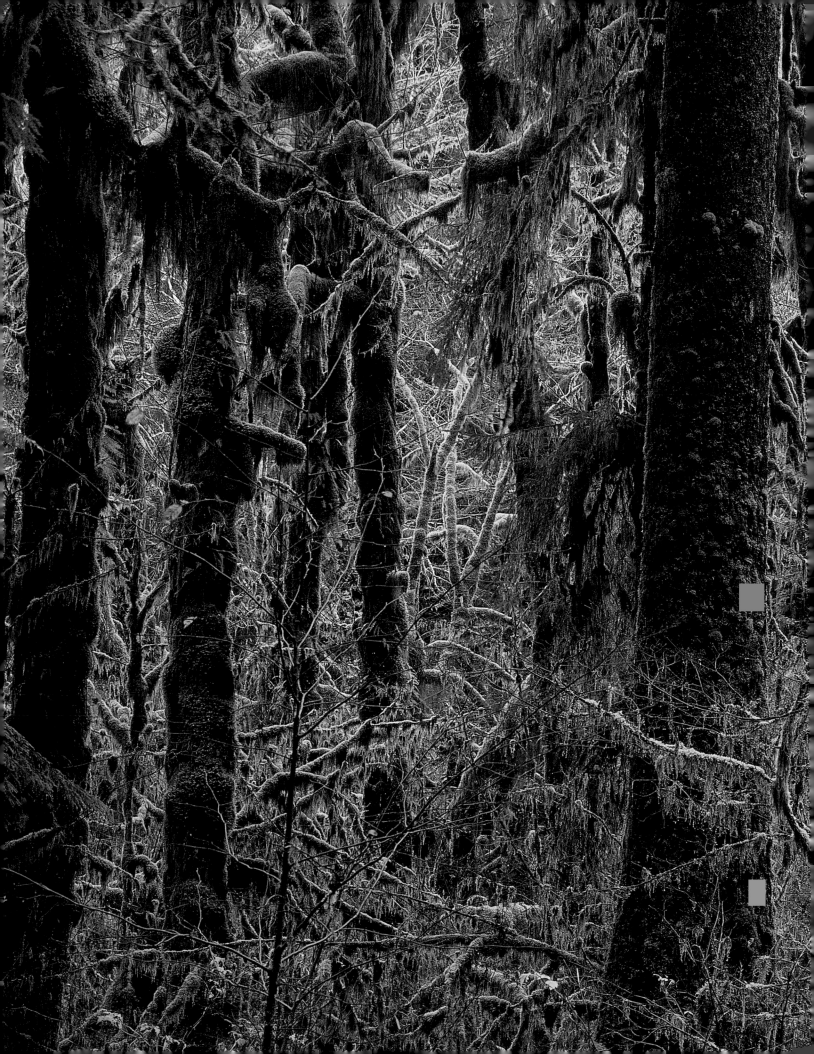

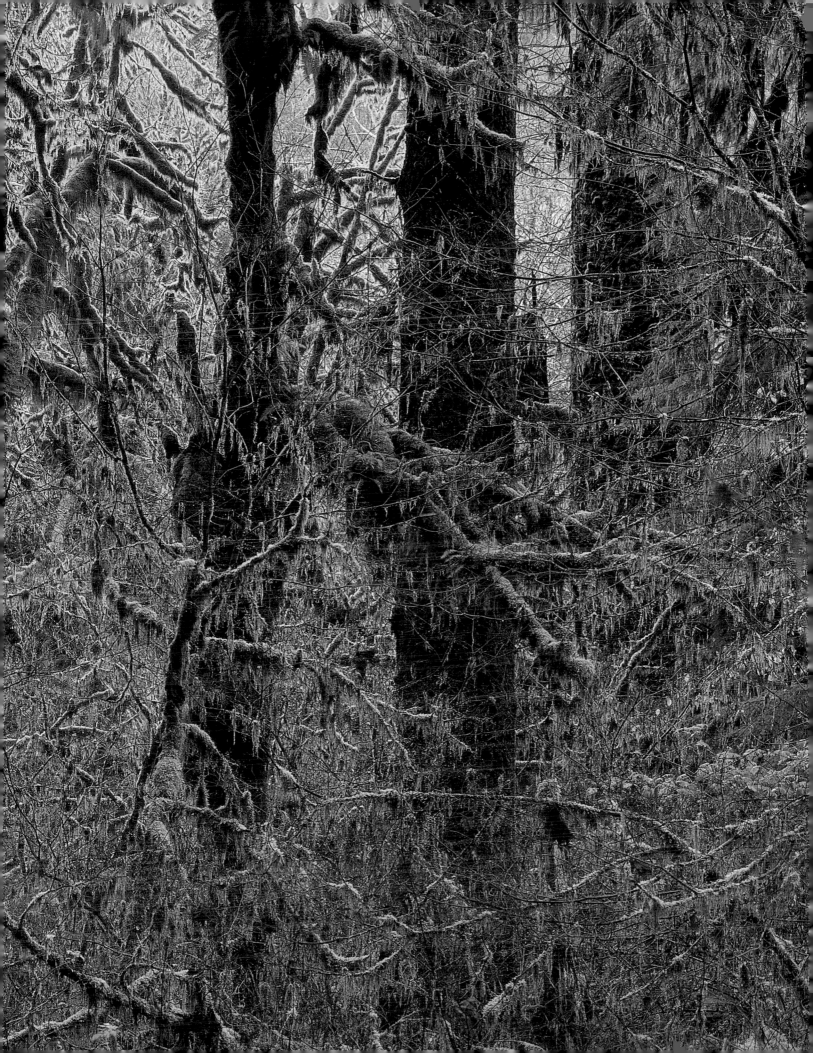

Below: Bunchberry dogwoods near Sequim, Washington

Right: Hoh River tributary, Olympic National Park, Washington

Following page: Coast redwoods, Prairie Creek Redwoods State Park, northern California

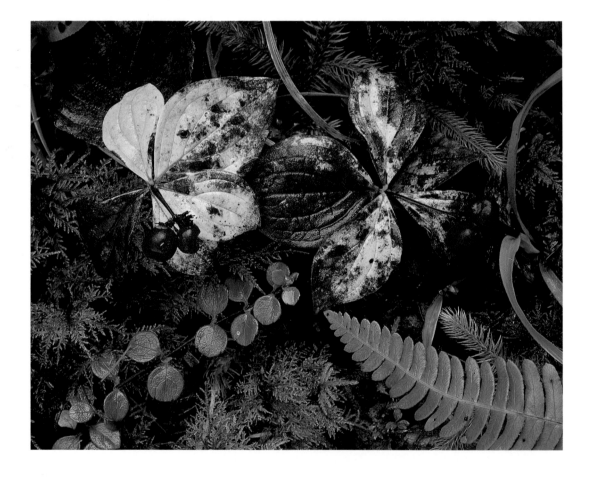

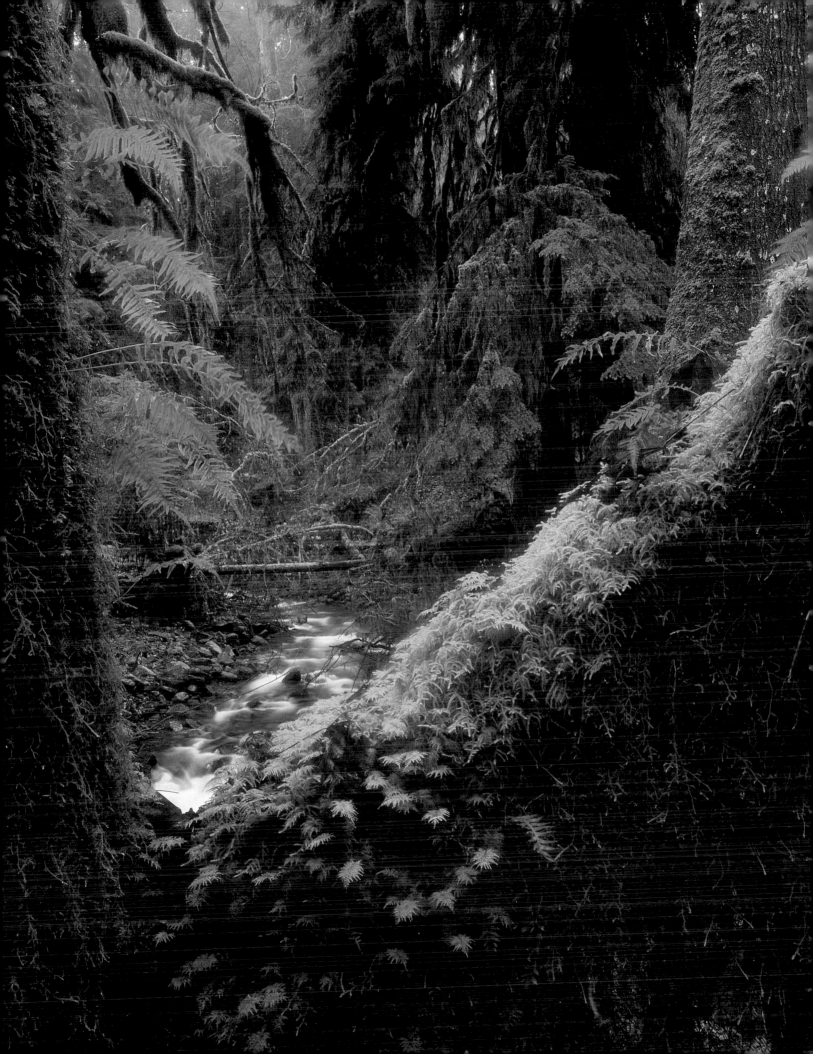

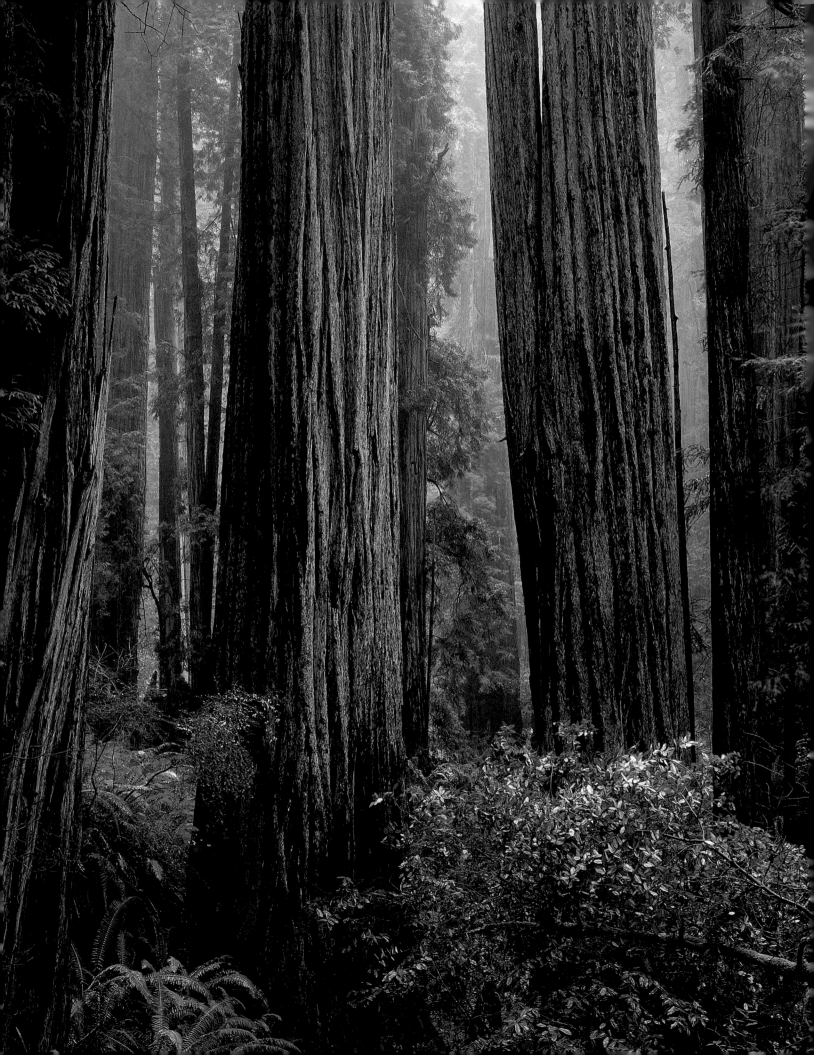

Walk into the rain forest
and sense time.

Trees that are centuries old soar three hundred feet high,

their trunks like pillars in a nave

and the light beneath them like that filtered through cathedral glass.

Ruth Kirk, "What Is the Rain Forest?"

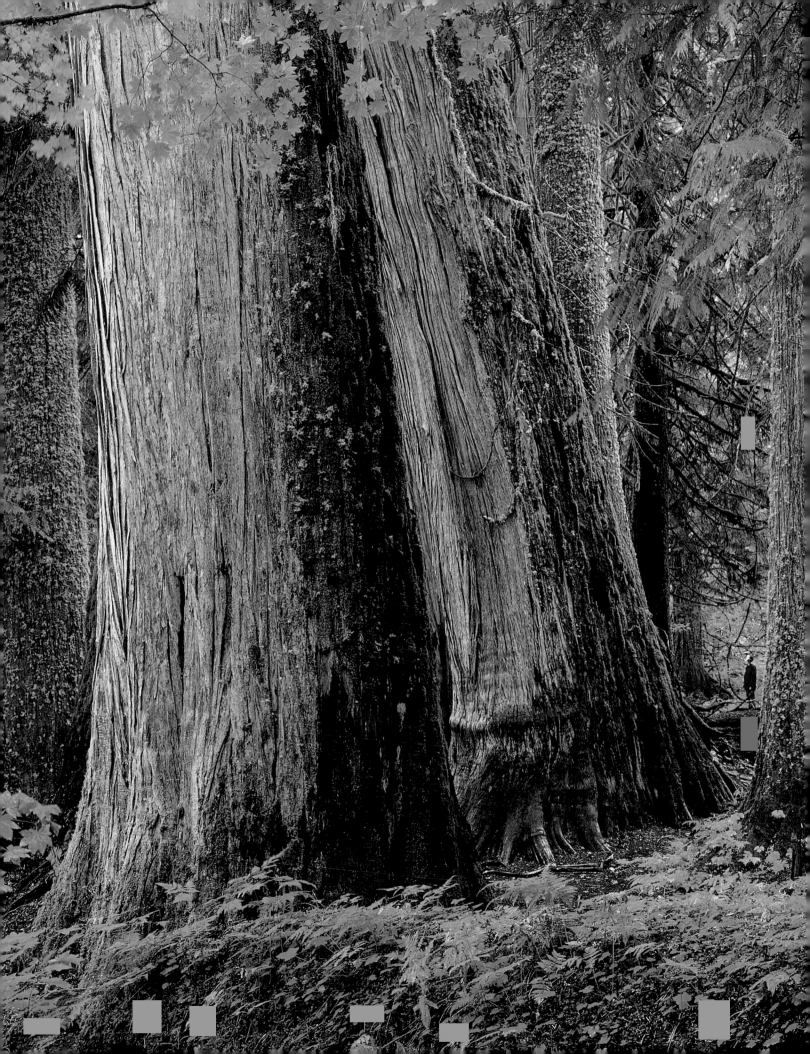

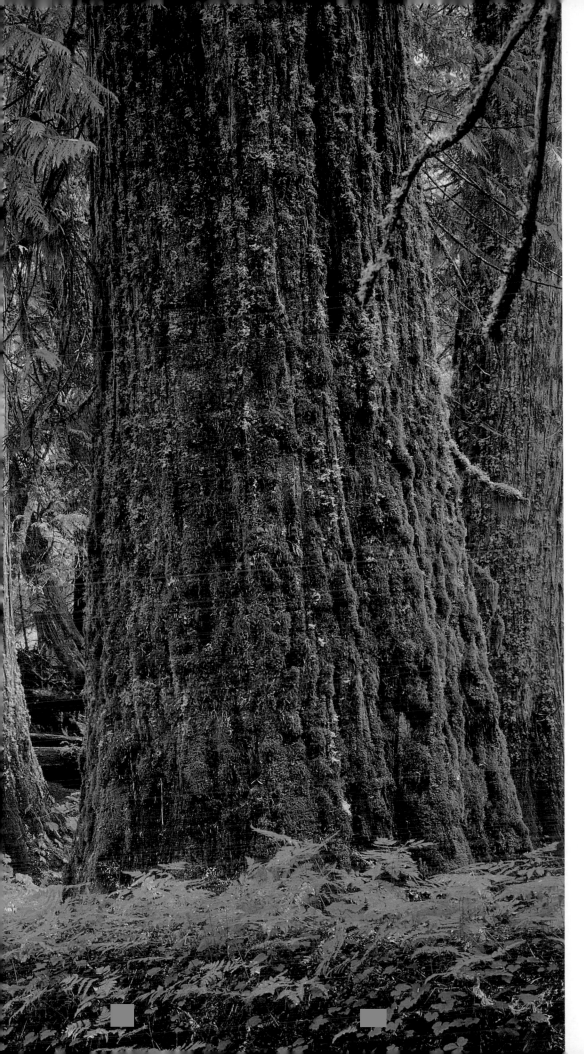

Grove of the Patriarchs,
Mt. Rainier National Park,
Washington

Overleaf: Big leaf maples,
Hall of Mosses, Olympic
National Park, Washington

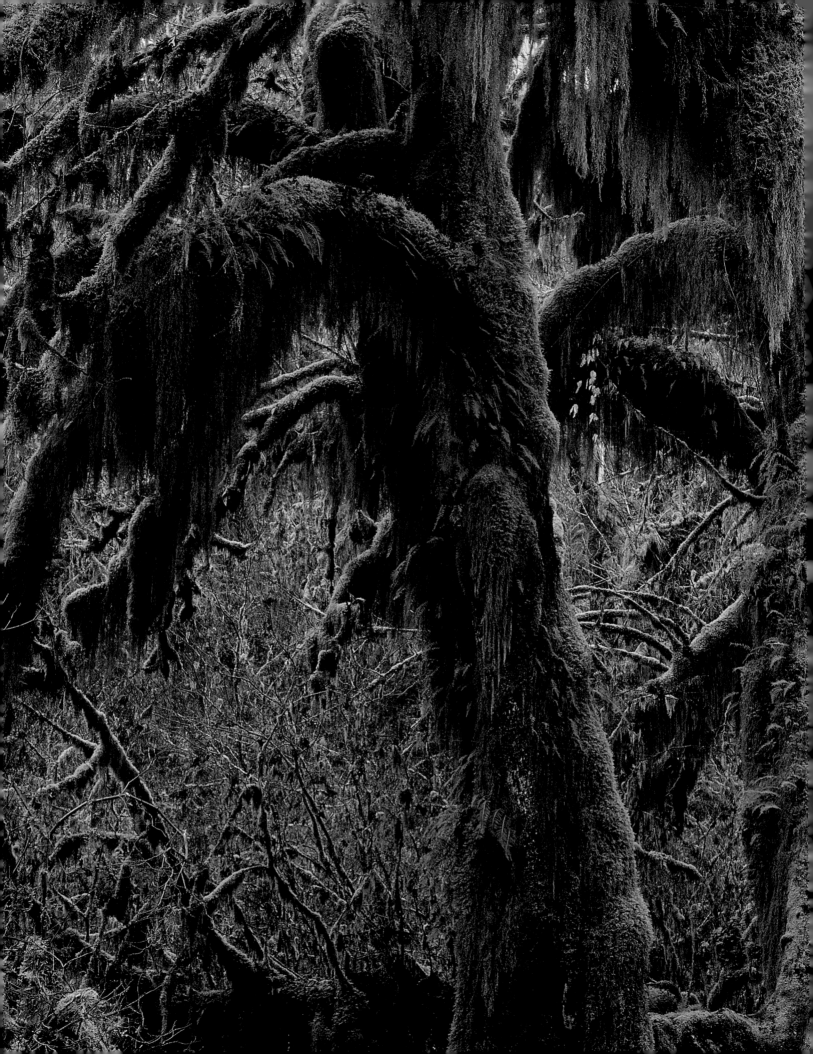

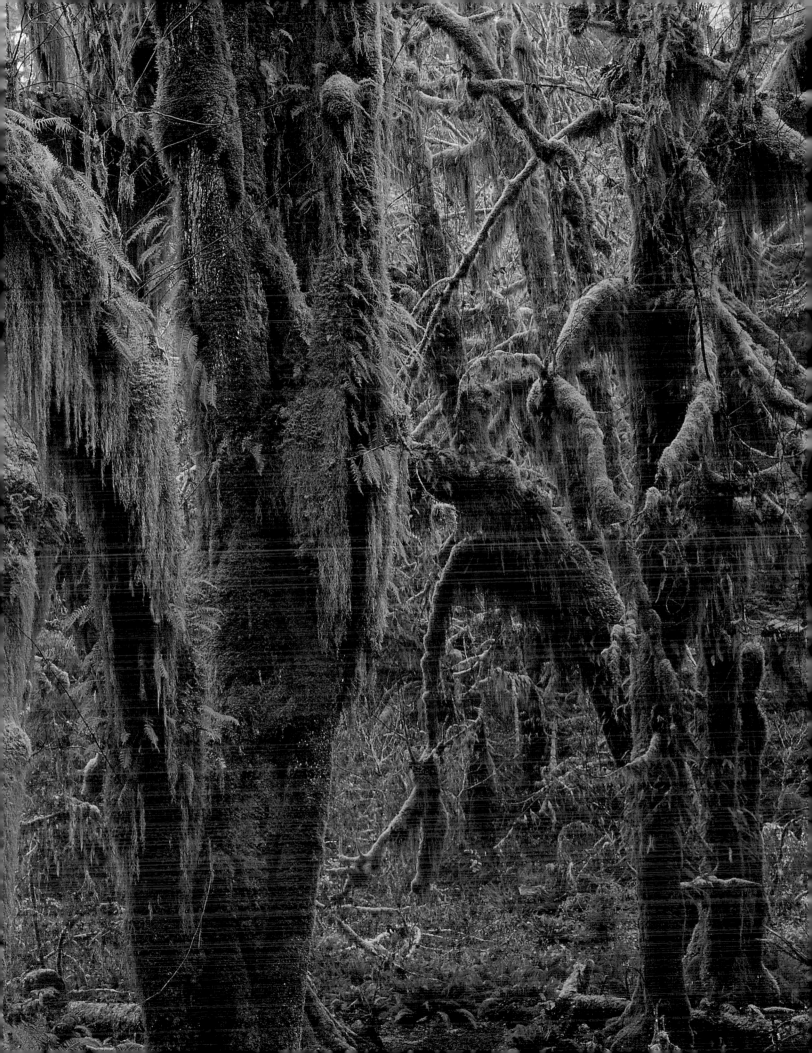

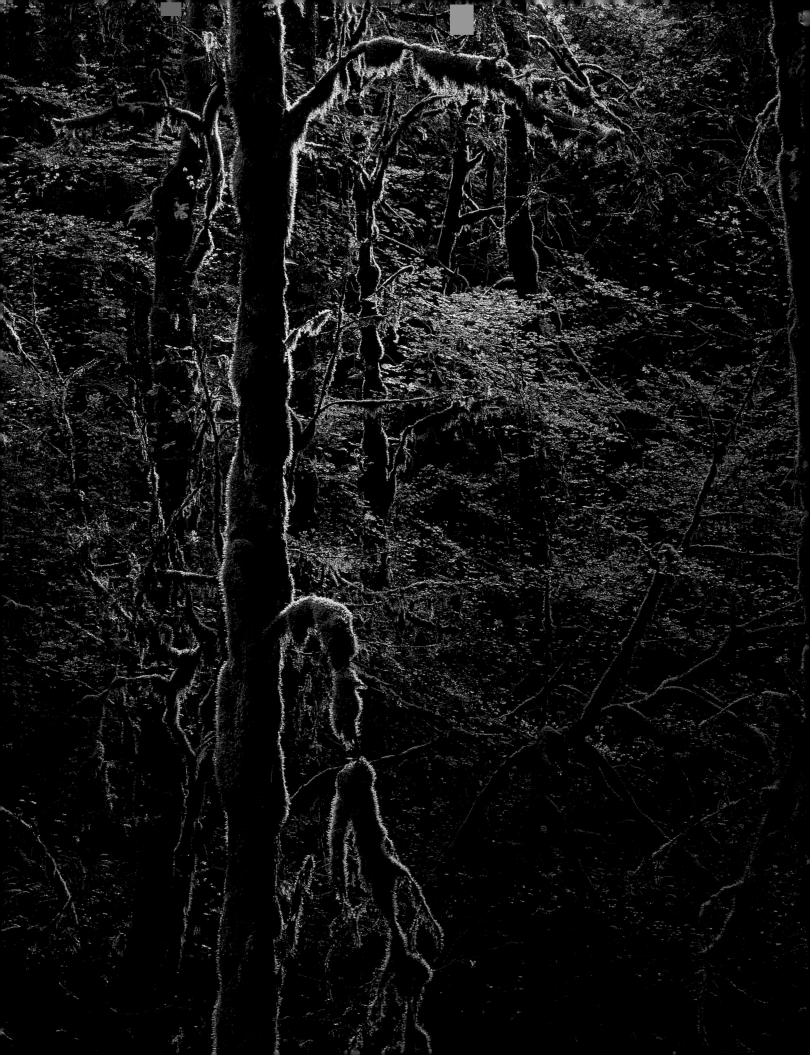

To Bryce Lien
Box 1124
9080 S. March Point Road
Unit B3
Anacortes Washington
98221

Hi Bryce, Rogue, Ryder, Kylie, Baloo and Minnie.

I finally got an address for you with the help of some friends. I was so sorry I never got in on the quilt for you as it was a secret and somehow I missed out on it. No matter, I have wanted to send these books to you for a while. I did p.m. you but I totally understand you not responding. You are a very private man and I respect and honor that. So I am using the H2O4K9 wharehouse address instead. It will work just fine.

The little map I put in the Vancouver Island book is to show you my area where I live. I was so surprised that Port McNeill was not on that map! We have around 2300 people living here. Such a wonderful place. Lots of fishing, camping, hiking, crabbing, and kayaking here. Fresh air and never too hot. So enjoy that book. The other one is of the Pacific Northwest where we live and so do you. Such awesome pictures I thought you would like this too.

I just want to let you know how much I feel so gifted and rewarded belonging to Happy Endings. I was there the day you got Rogue and have been part of the group you formed since day one pretty much. I have never met such a loving and friendly bunch of people as I have with this group. I look forward to each day reading about everyone and their fur babies and what is going on in their lives. Love your fur love bubies and feel like they are family. I have freinded a lot of the group and hope one day to meet up with some of them. If we ever come down your way on a camping trip, I will definitely look you up. The same goes for you if you ever make the trip to the Island. Let me know and hubby and I could meet you part way. We are around four hours north once the ferry lands in Nanaimo. Long way to drive.

So I leave you with lots of hugs and looking forward to updates on your new place. It looks so lovely.

Lots of hugs and much love   pmacdermid@gmail.com

Pauline MacDermid .. Box 1051, Port McNeill, B.C. V0N 2R0, CANADA

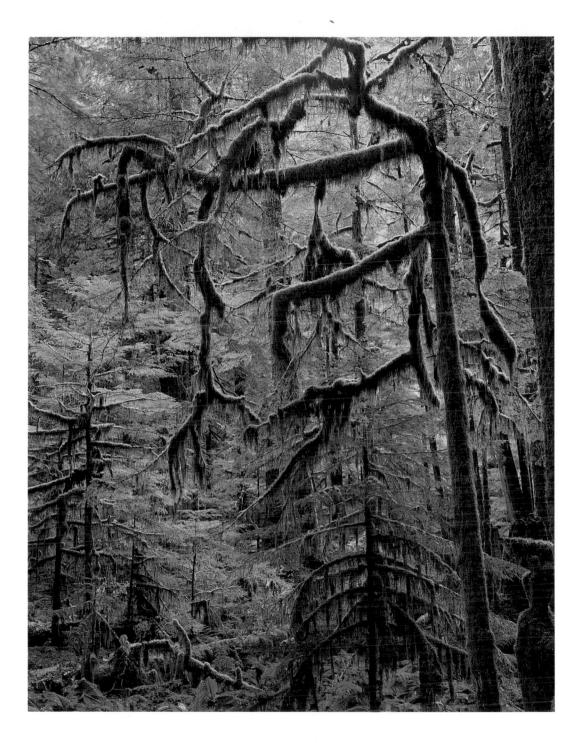

Facing page: Elwha Valley, Washington

Above: Carbon River rainforest, Mt. Rainier National Park, Washington

Overleaf: Coltsfoot growing along a rainforest creek near Chilliwack Lake, British Columbia

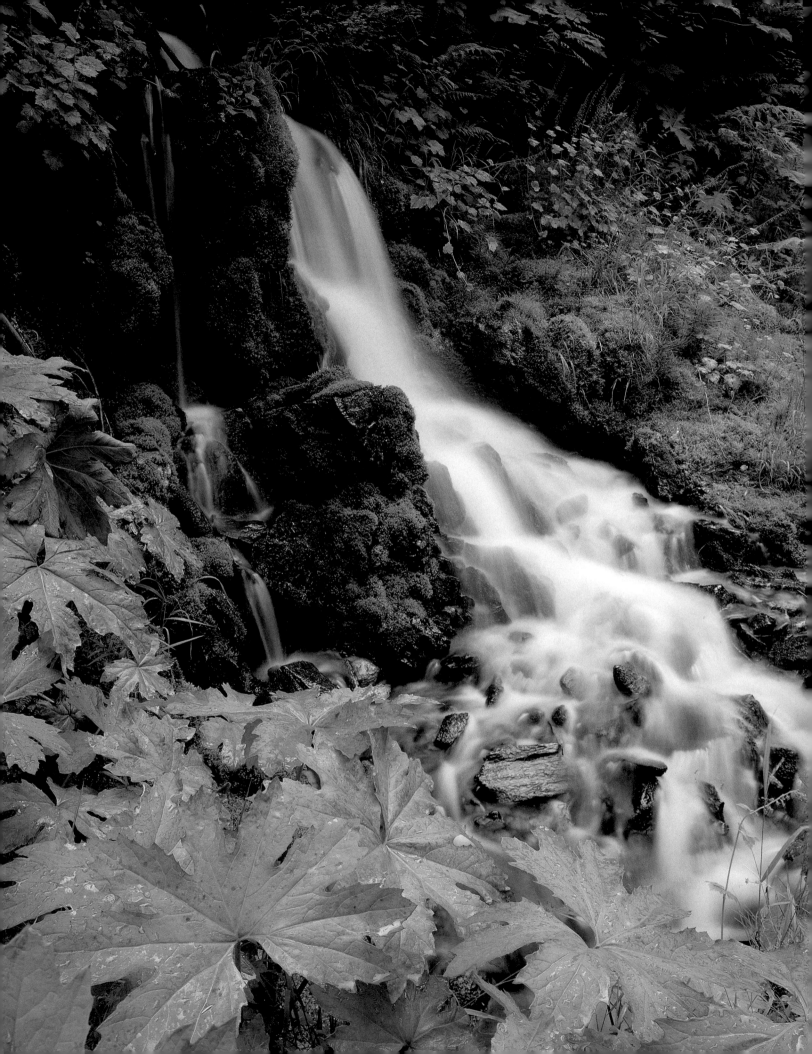

The streams *which thread the Pacific forest*

tie the land to the sea in an inseparable relationship.

Nowhere on the continent are the forest and its inhabitants

more dependent upon water. . . .

Gerry Ellis and Karen Kane, "An Evergreen Oasis"

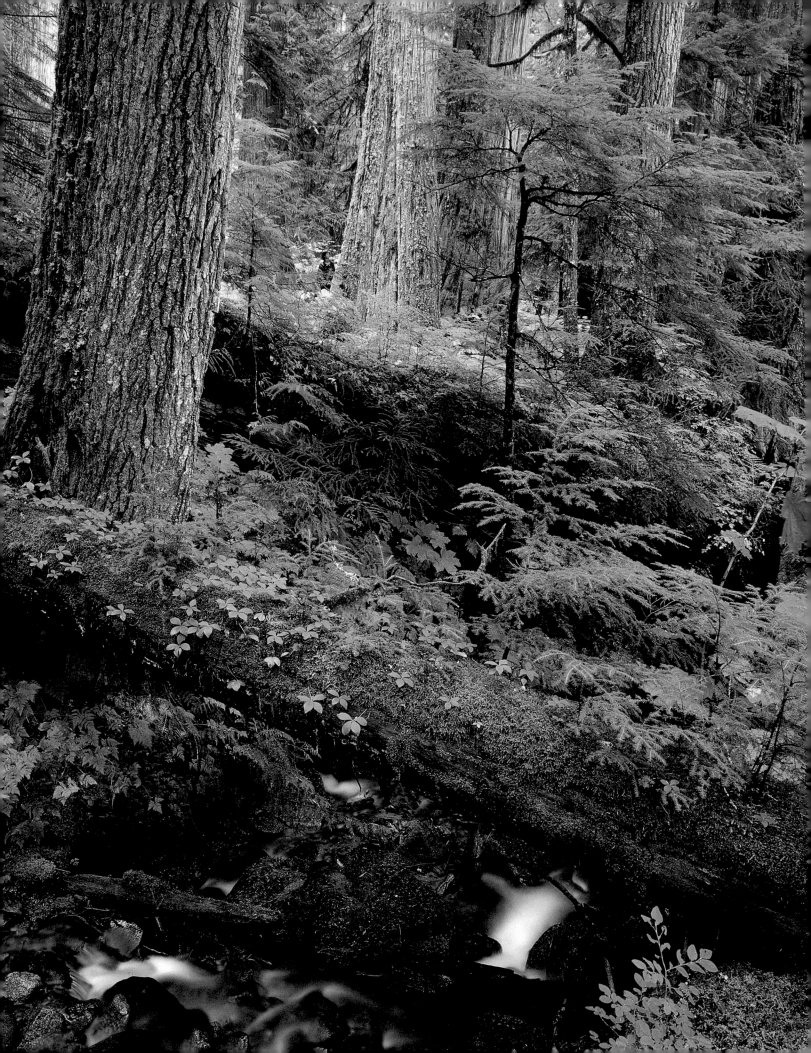

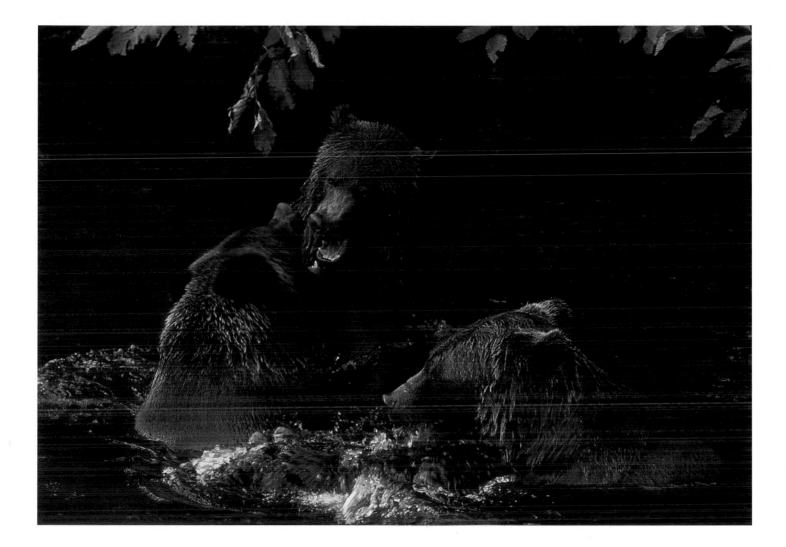

*Facing page: Grove of giant
cedars and hemlocks, Stoltmann
Wilderness, upper Elaho River,
British Columbia*

*Above: Grizzlies wrestling along
a coastal spawning stream, Knight
Inlet, British Columbia*

*Overleaf: A pair of spawning
sockeye salmon, Fraser River
watershed, British Columbia*

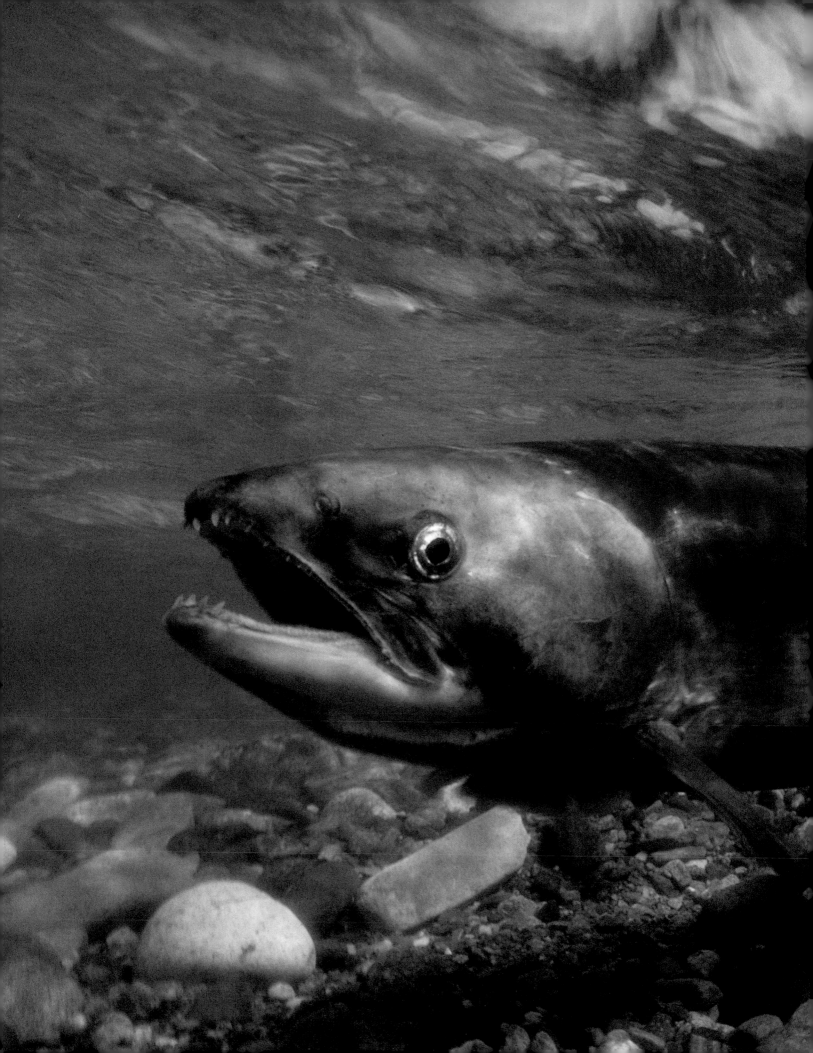

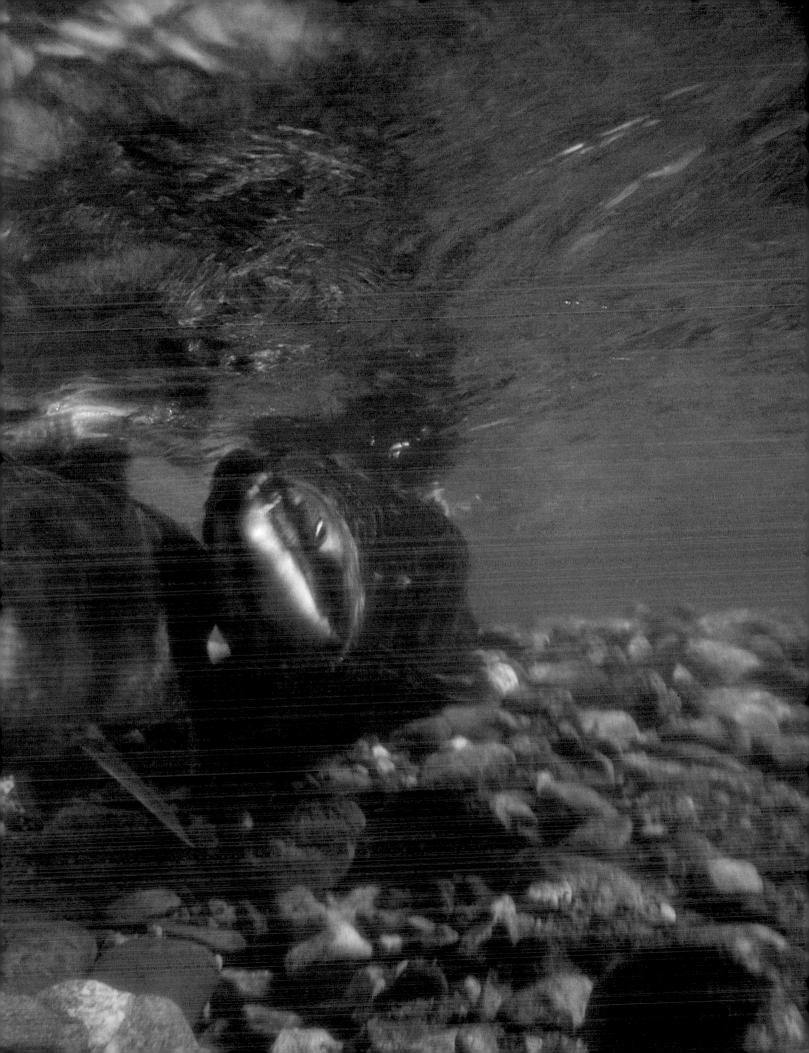

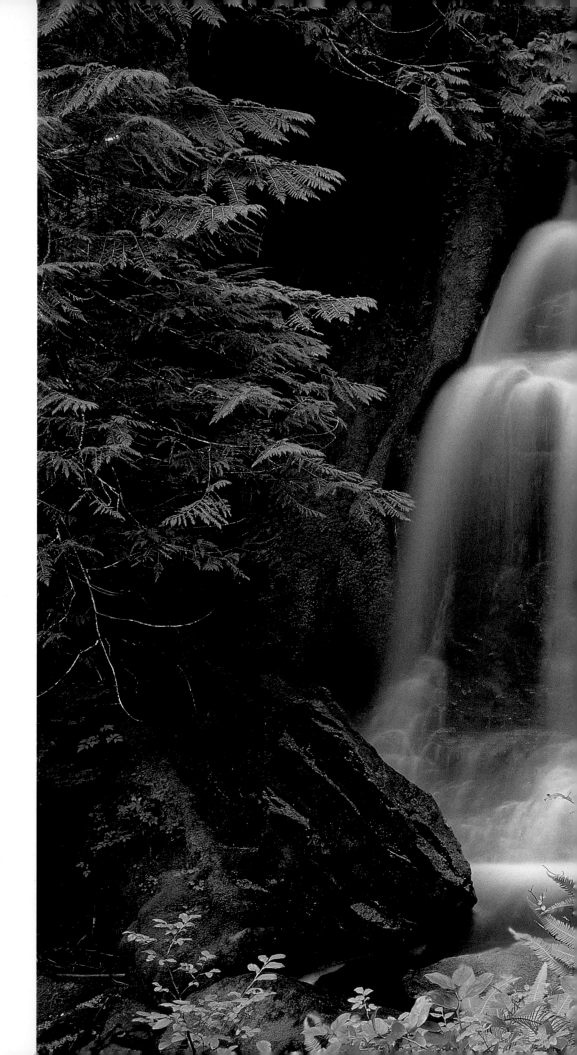

Waterfall in the Ellerslie Valley,
midcoast of British Columbia

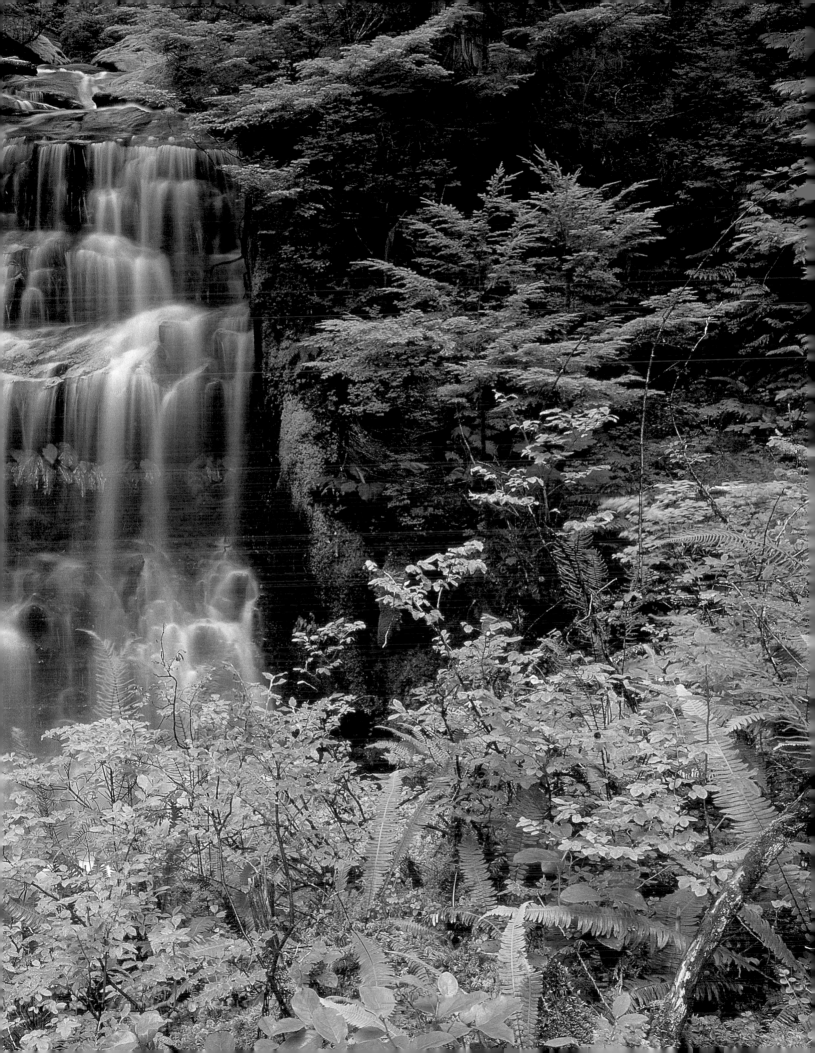

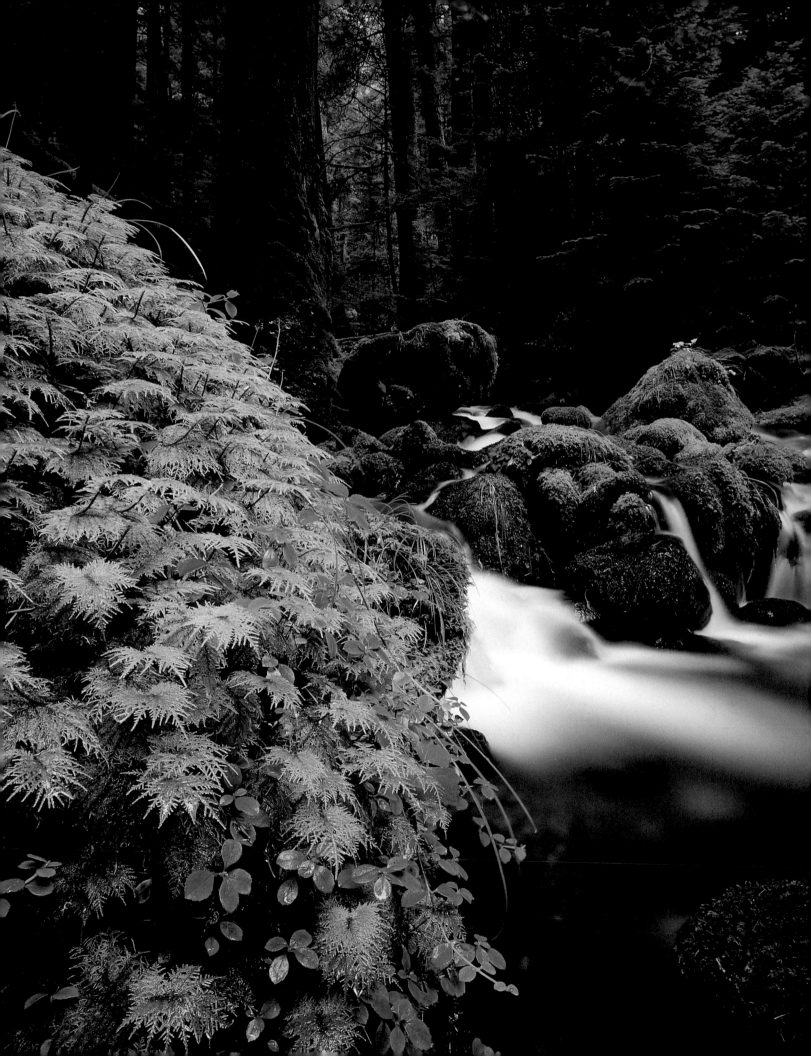

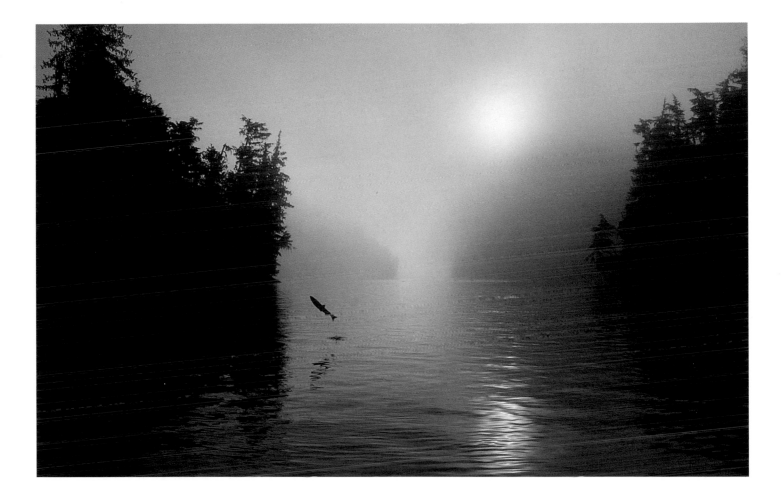

Facing page: A rainforest creek near Port Angeles, Washington

Above: A salmon leaping at first light, Koeye estuary near Bella Bella, British Columbia

Overleaf: Dolomite Narrows in Gwaii Haanas National Park, Queen Charlotte Islands, British Columbia

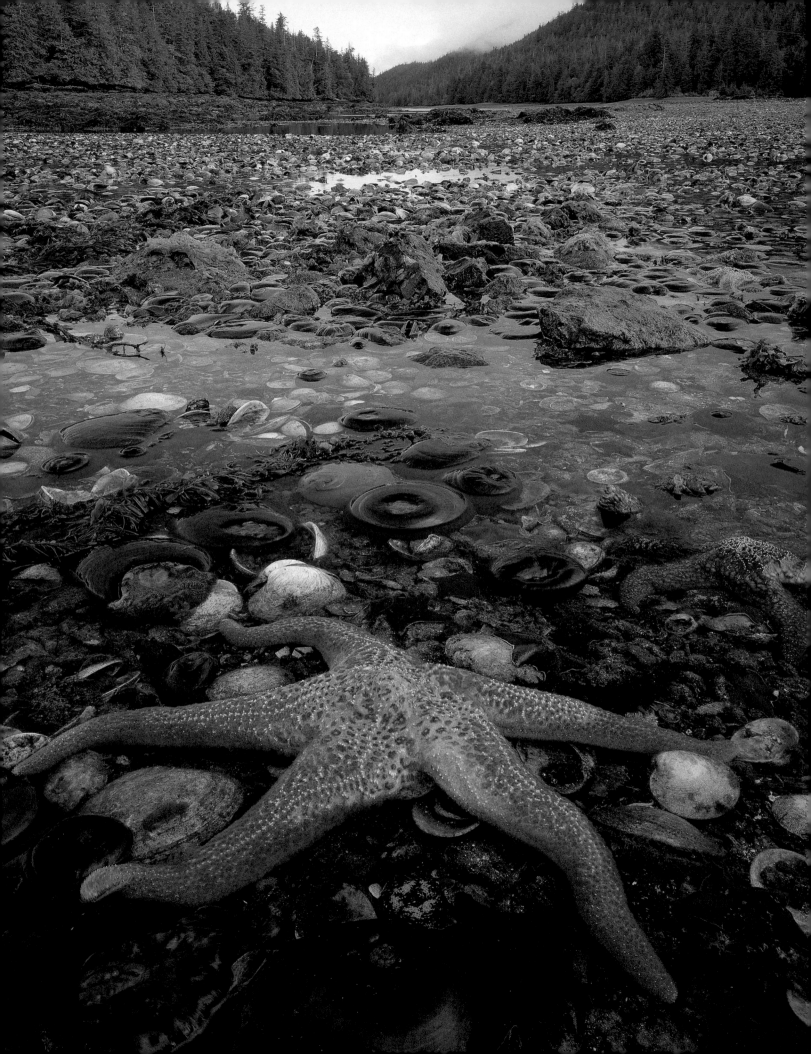

...the edge of the continent

is thick with life:

one cubic foot of tidepool can support

more than four thousand living things.

Timothy Egan, *The Good Rain: Across Time and Terrain in the Pacific Northwest*

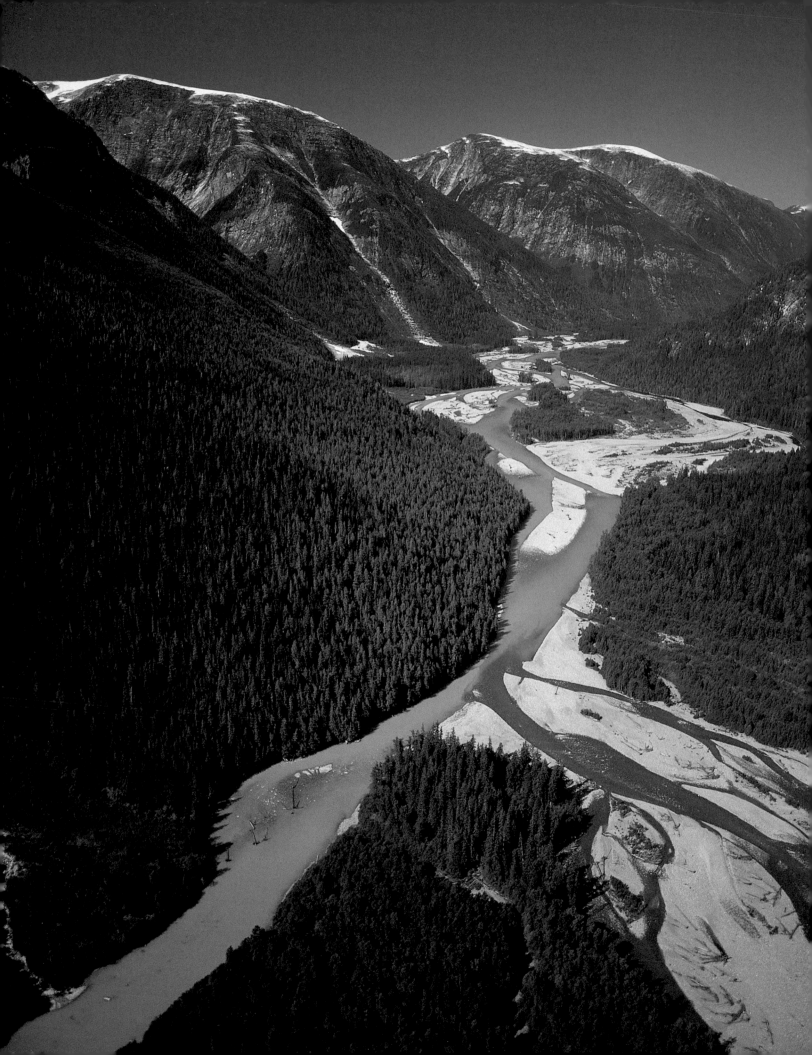

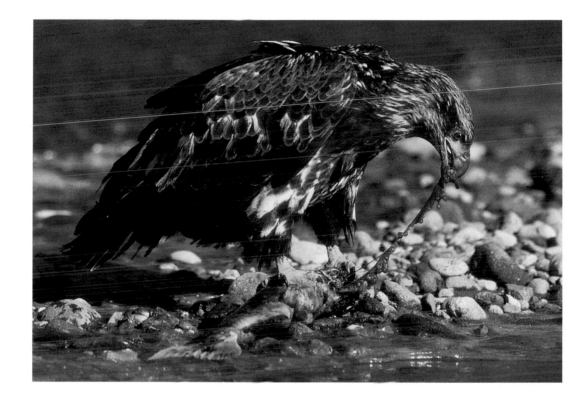

*Facing page: The Kitlope River
at its confluence with the Gamsby
River, British Columbia*

*Above: Immature bald eagle feed-
ing on coho salmon roe, Squamish
River, British Columbia*

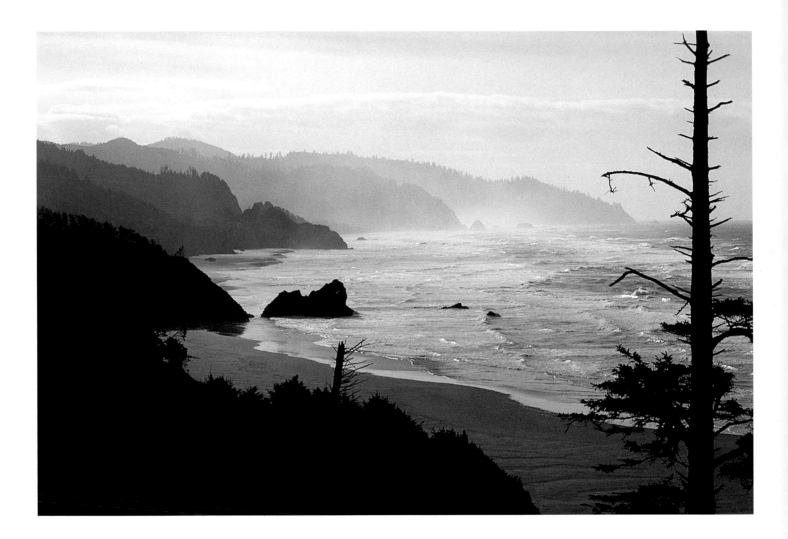

Above: The Oregon coast near Cannon Beach

Facing page: Sea stacks capped with old growth, near Sand Point, Olympic National Park, Washington

Following page: An unnamed rainforest creek in Olympic National Park, near Port Angeles, Washington

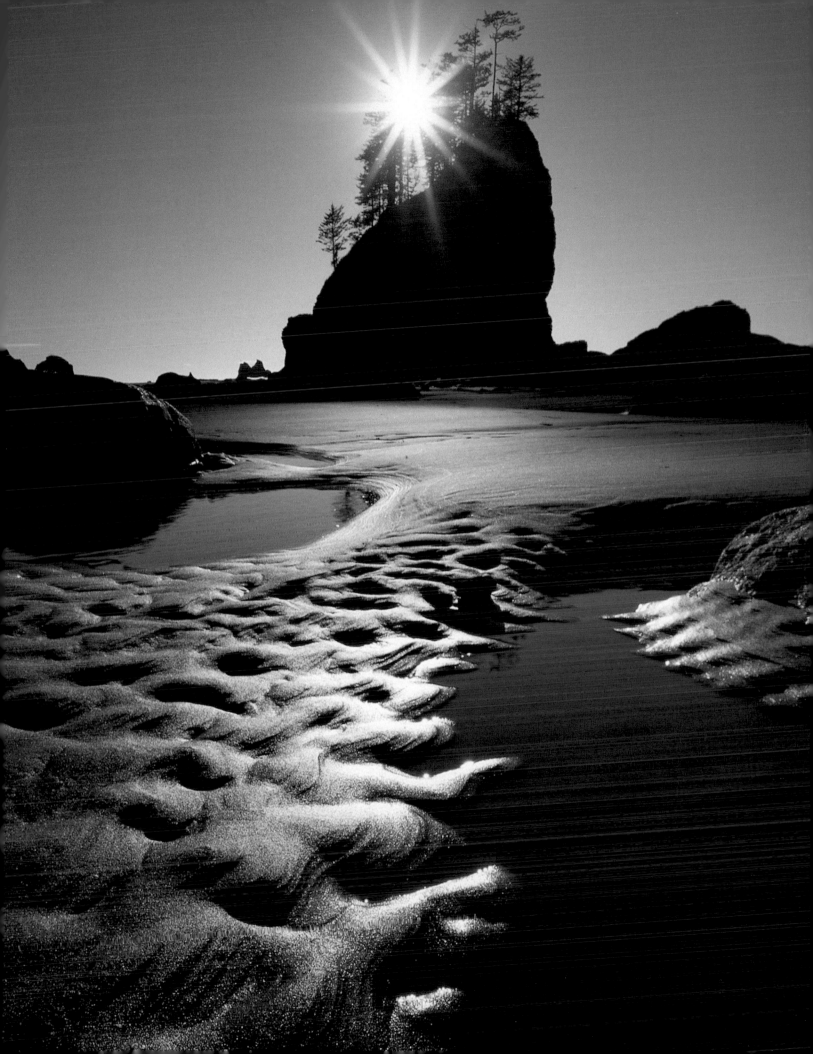

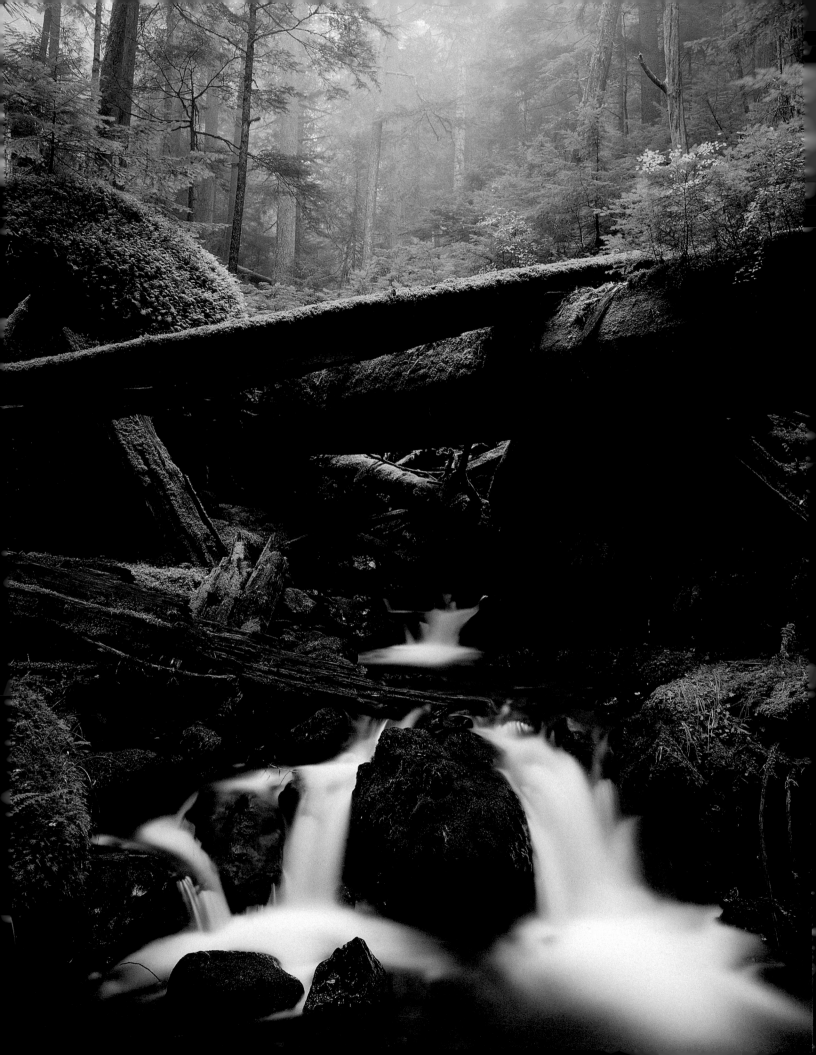

As you walk into these forests from the beach, the environment quickly changes from open, bright, and noisy to cool and serene, humid and dark.

Paul Alaback and Jim Pojar, "Vegetation from Ridgetop to Seashore"

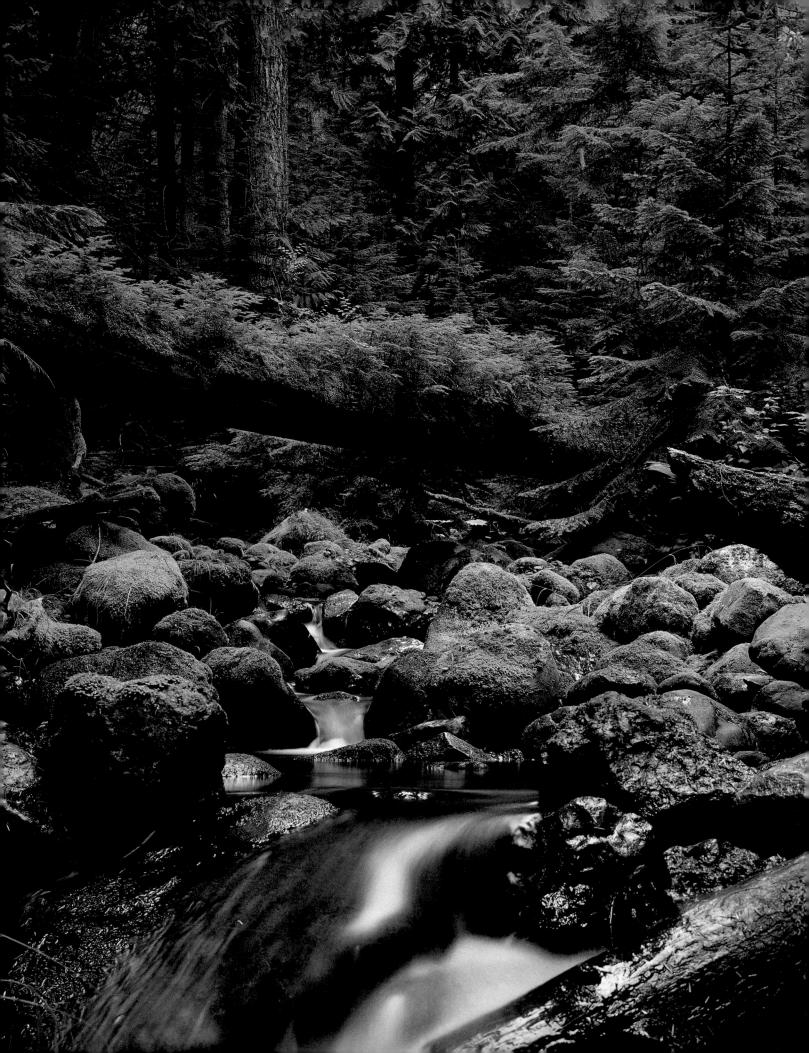

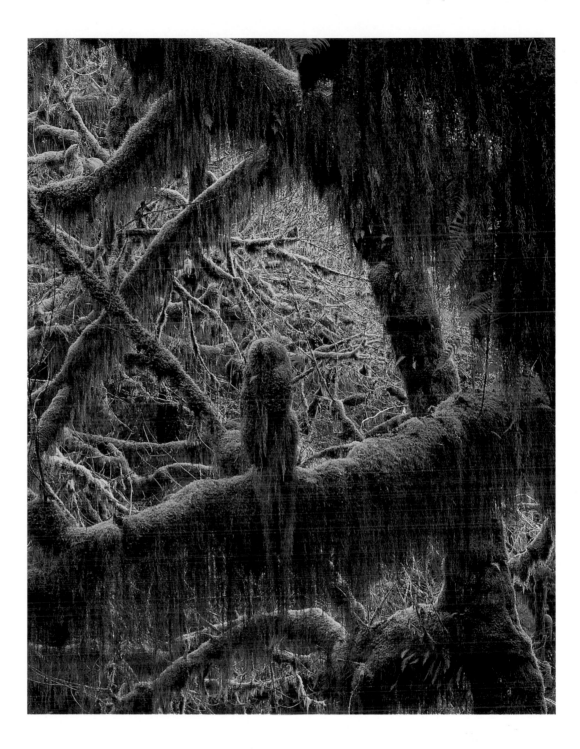

Facing page: Creek and nurse log, Nitinat Triangle, Vancouver Island, British Columbia

Above: Moss-draped big leaf maples near the Bogachiel River, Washington

Overleaf: Vine maples near Lake Mills, Olympic National Park, Washington

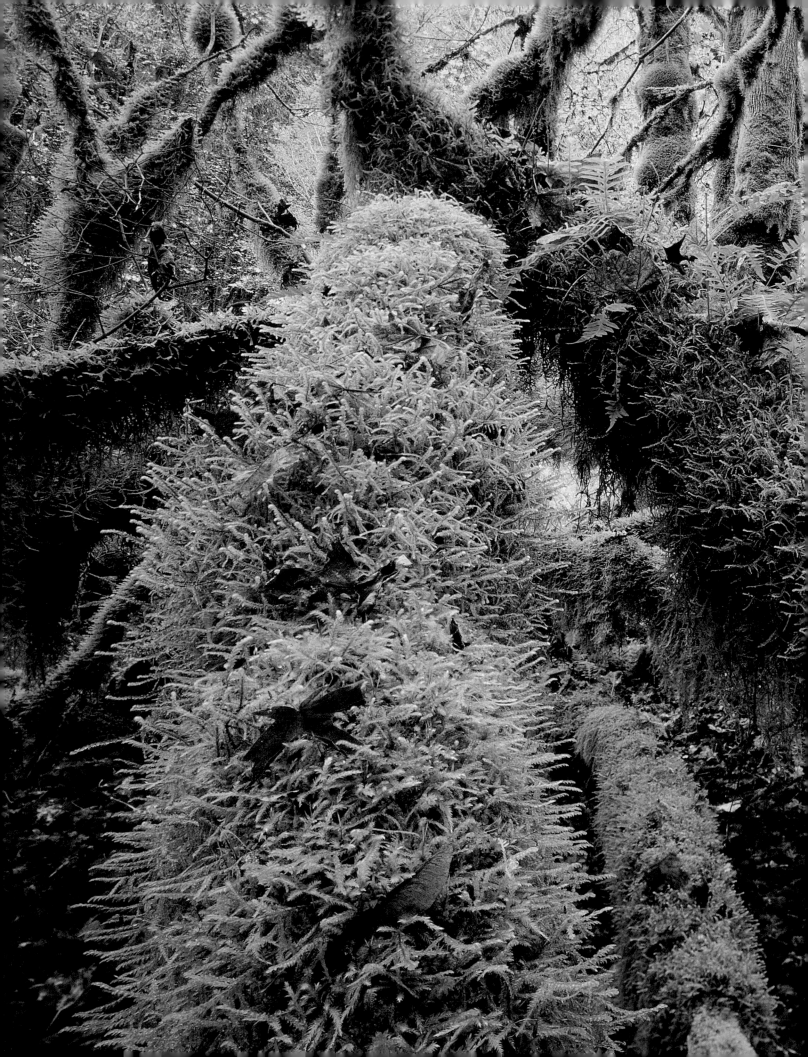

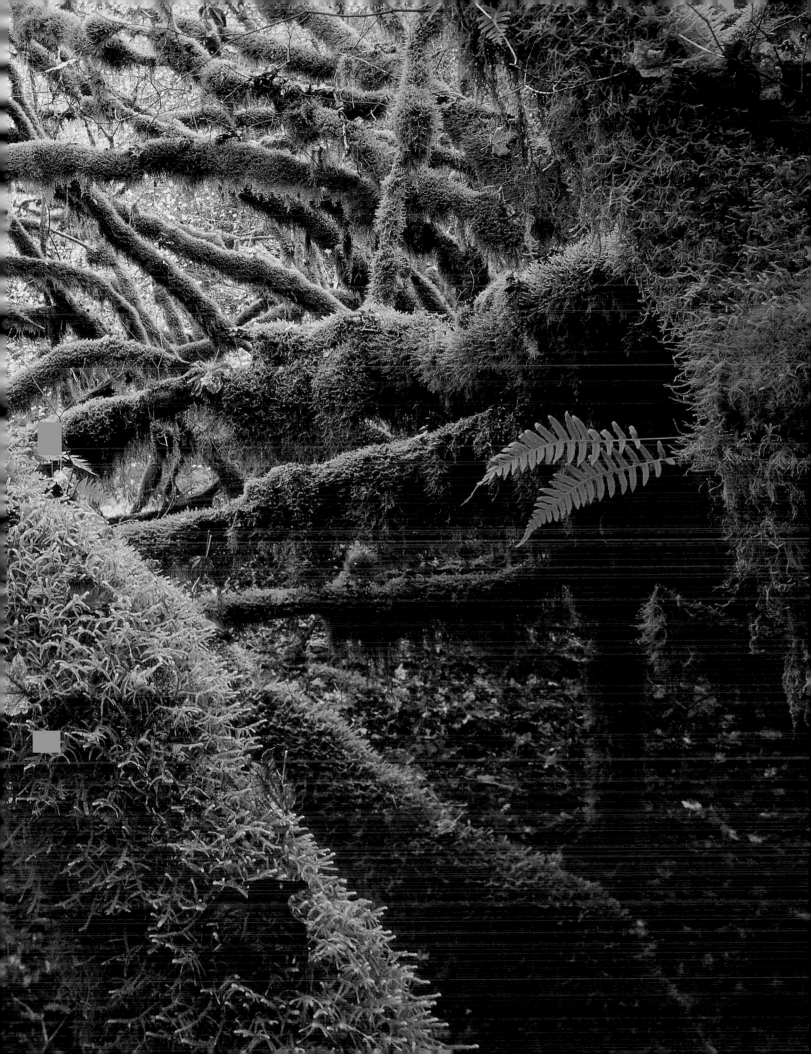

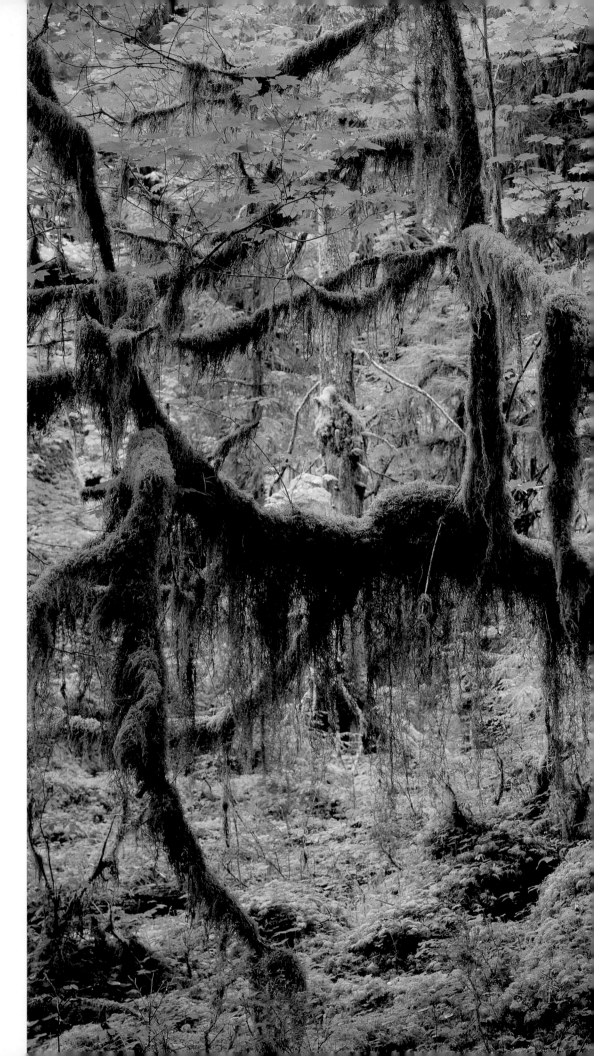

Giant Sitka spruce, Hoh River Valley, Olympic National Park, Washington

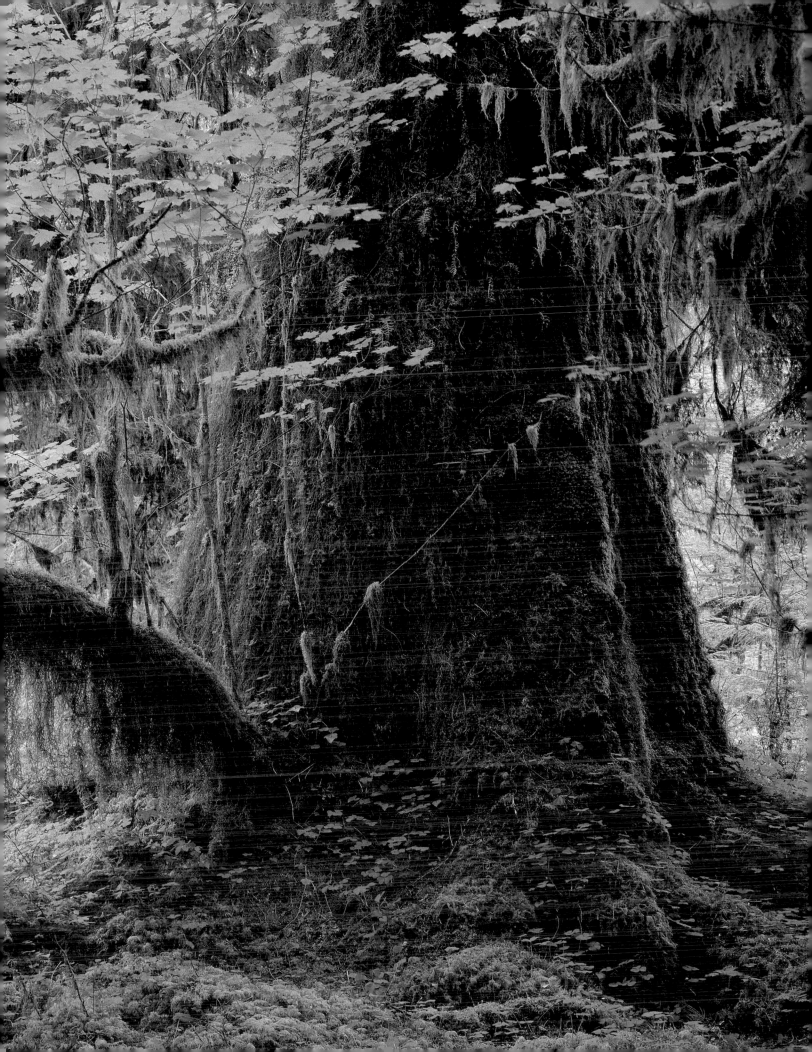

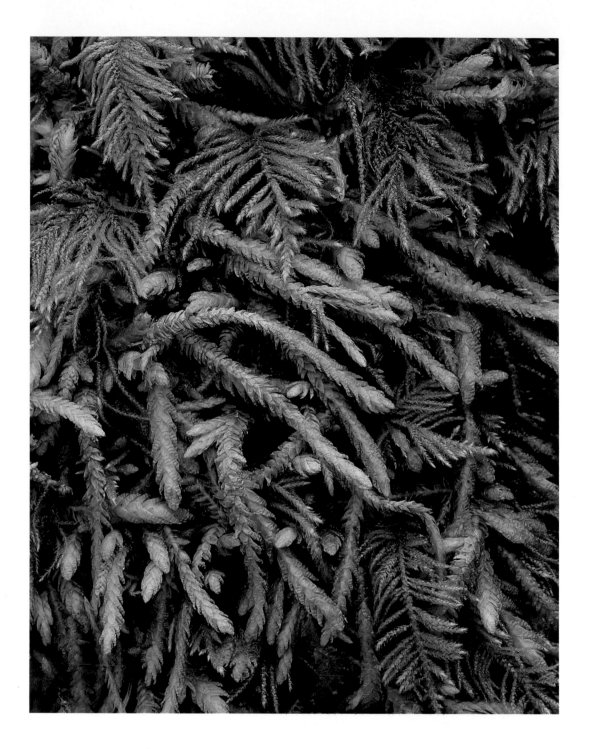

*Above: Forest floor mosses near
Rennell Sound, in the Queen
Charlotte Islands, British
Columbia*

*Facing page: Big leaf maples,
Hall of Mosses, Olympic
National Park, Washington*

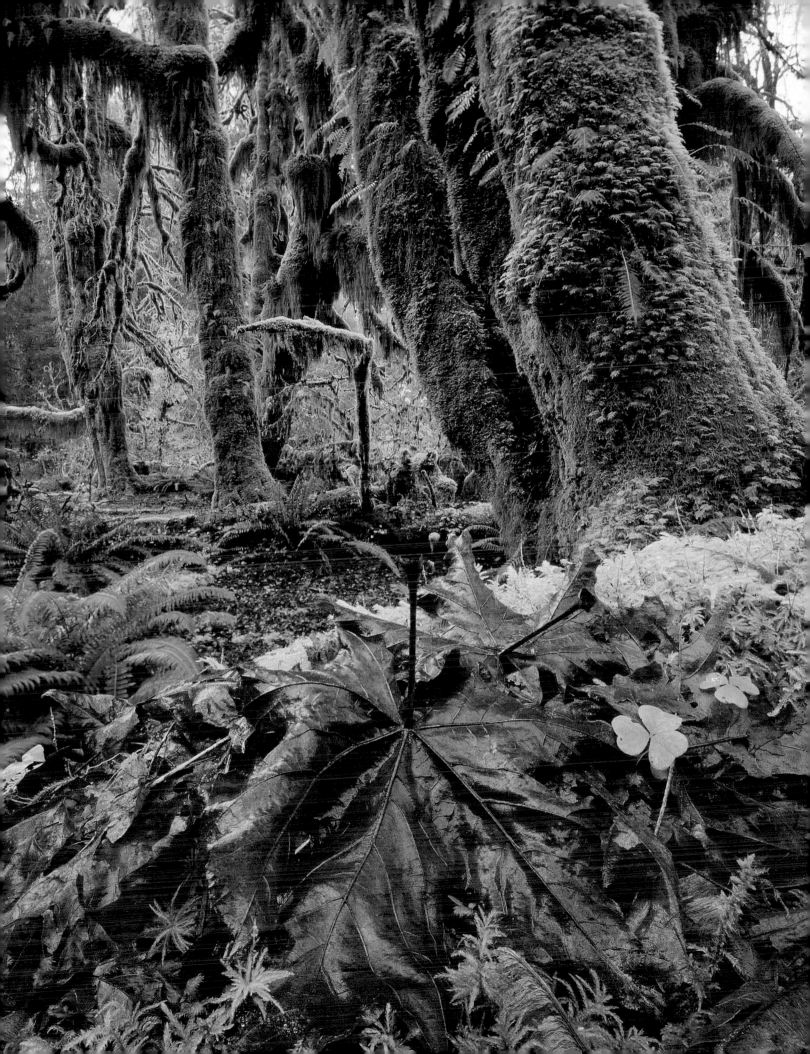

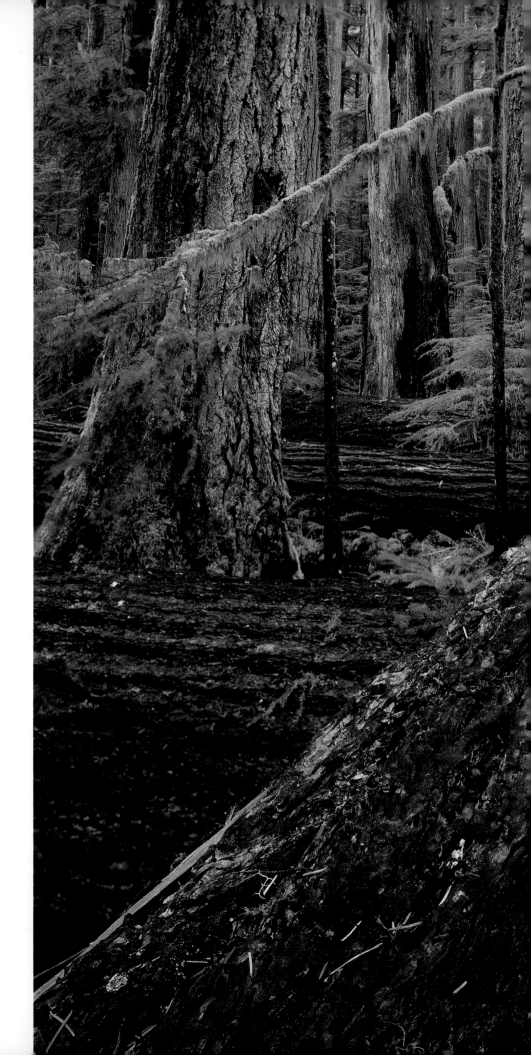

Douglas fir blowdown, Cathedral Grove, MacMillan Provincial Park, British Columbia

Following page: An ancient Douglas fir trunk festooned with lichens near Stevens Canyon, Mt. Rainier National Park, Washington

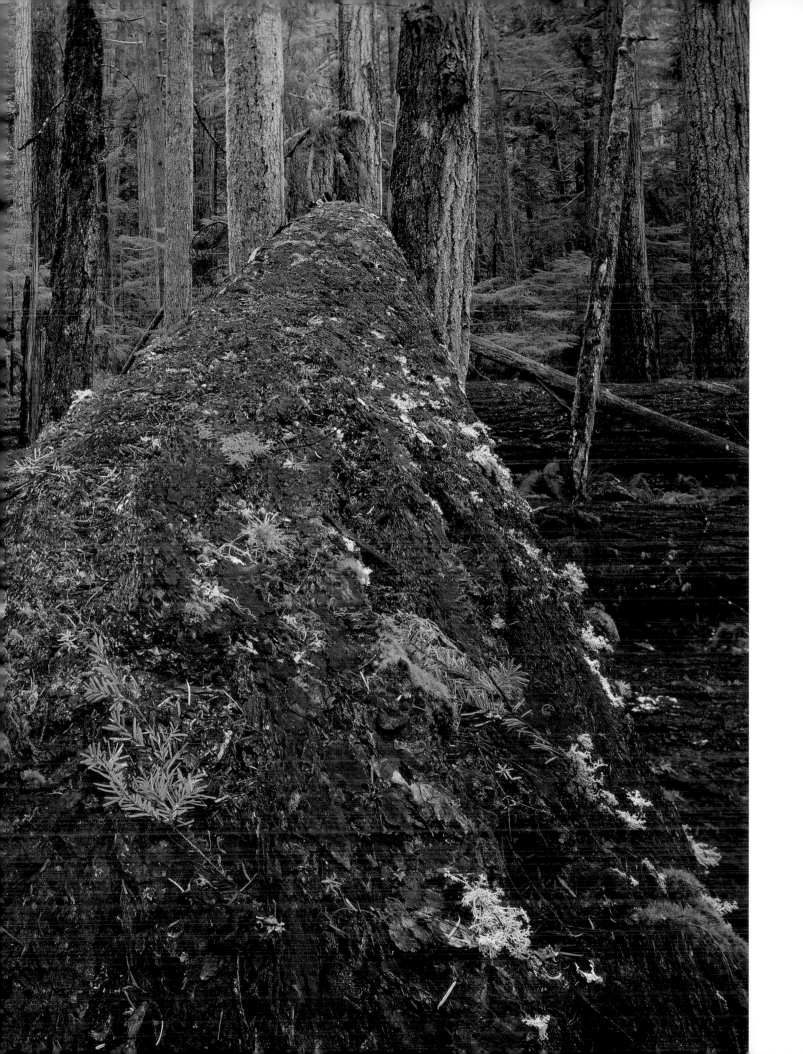

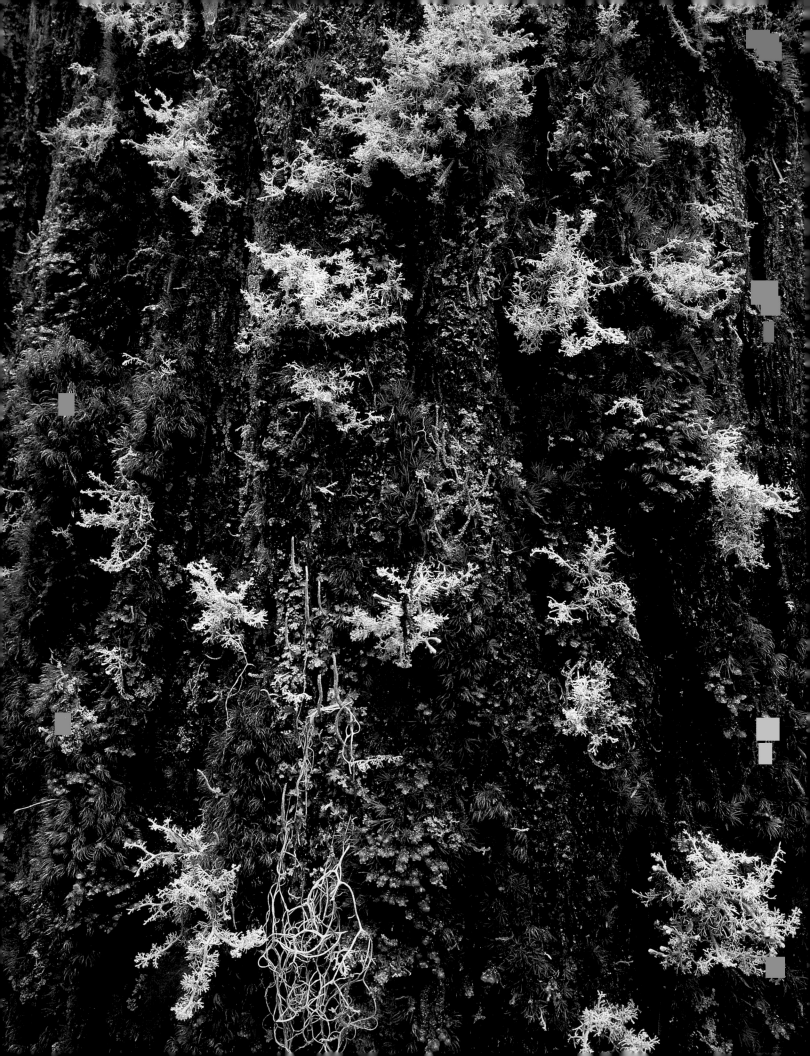

The quantity of life

in the Pacific rain forest is overwhelming.

Things grow everywhere: on branches two hundred feet in the air,

off the side of living trees, out of rotting stumps.

Gerry Ellis and Karen Kane, "The Forest and the Trees"

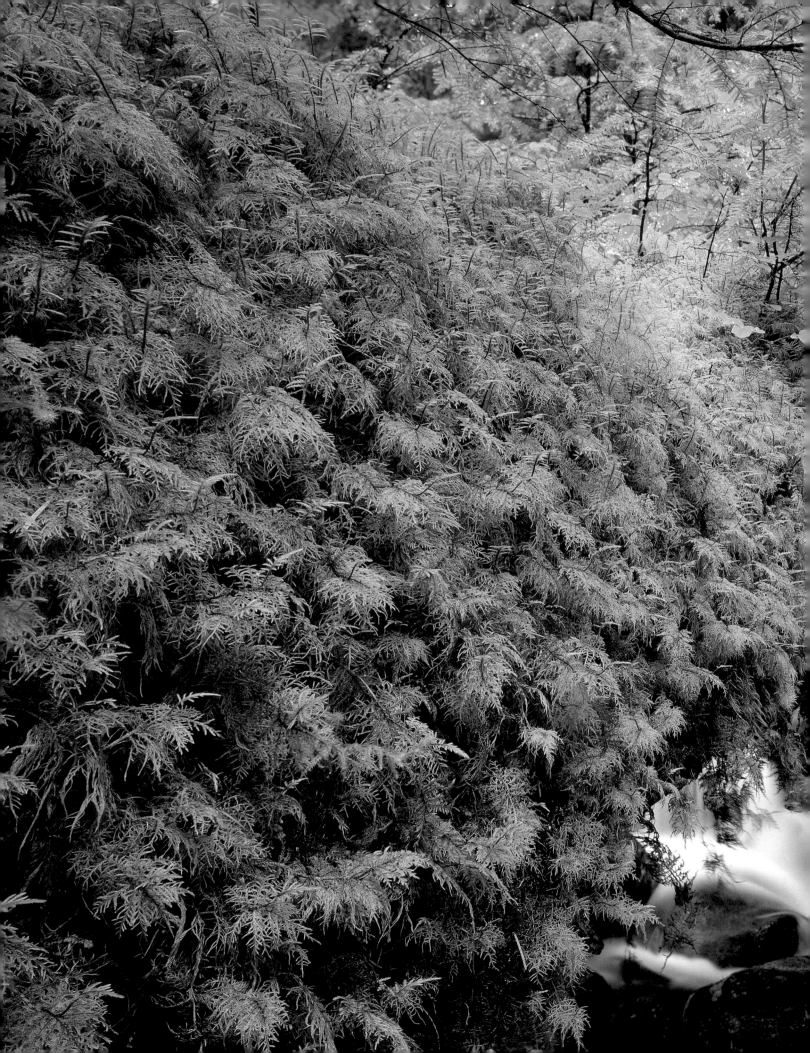

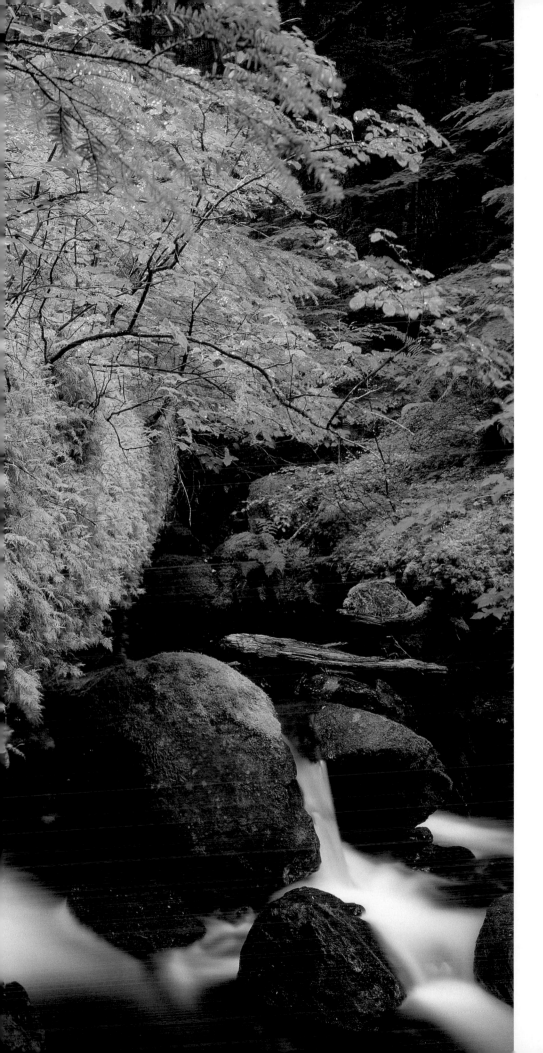

A nurse log carpeted with moss along the Ohanapecosh River, Washington

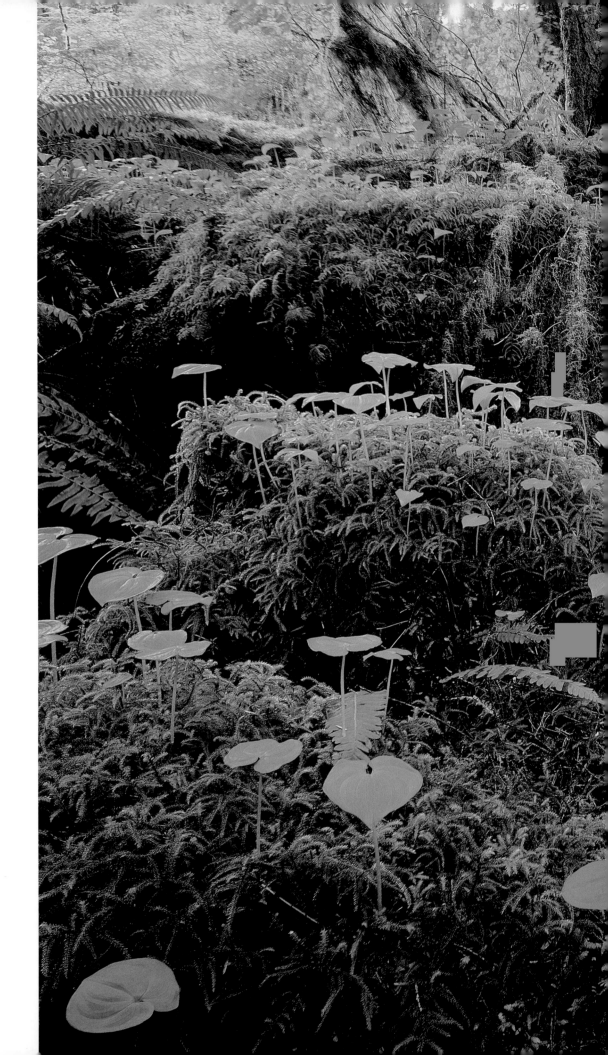

Moss and false lily of the valley gracing the forest floor of Sydney Valley, Clayoquot Sound, British Columbia

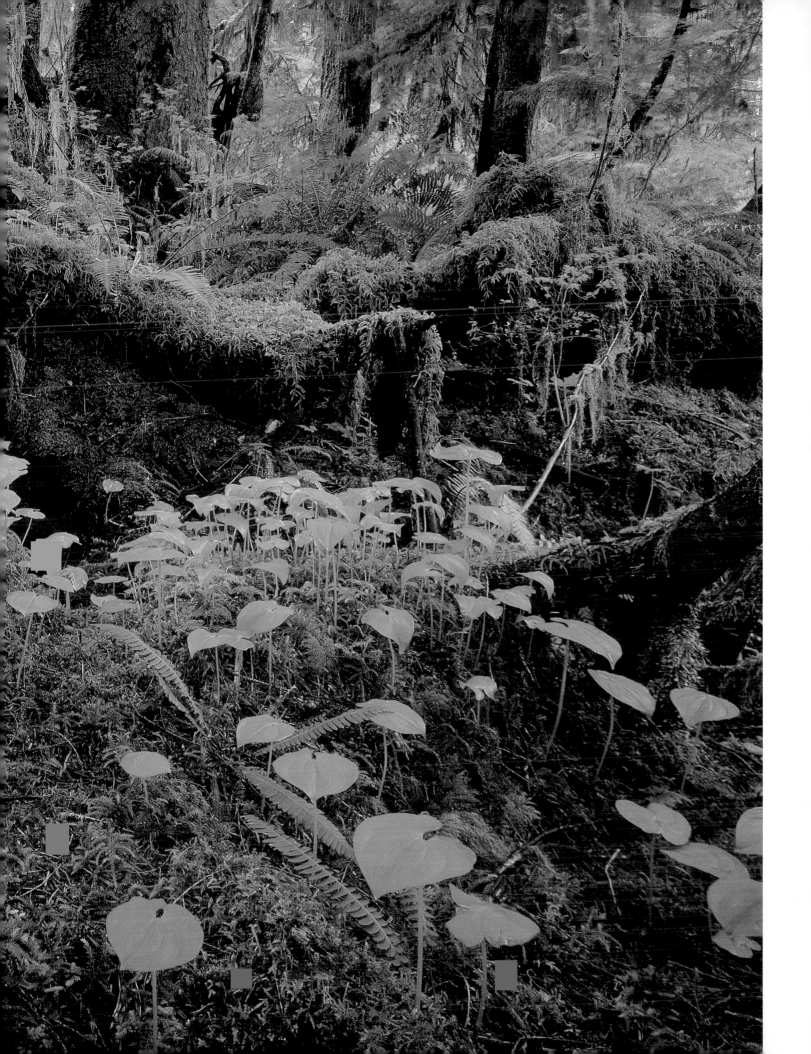

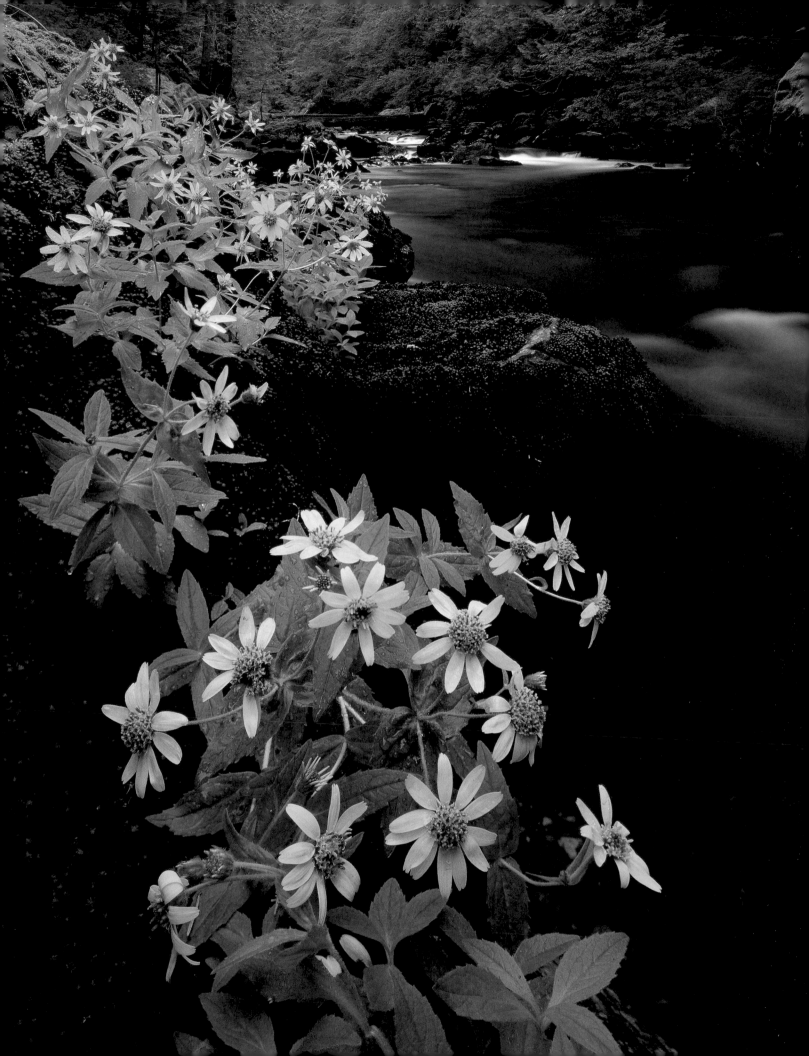

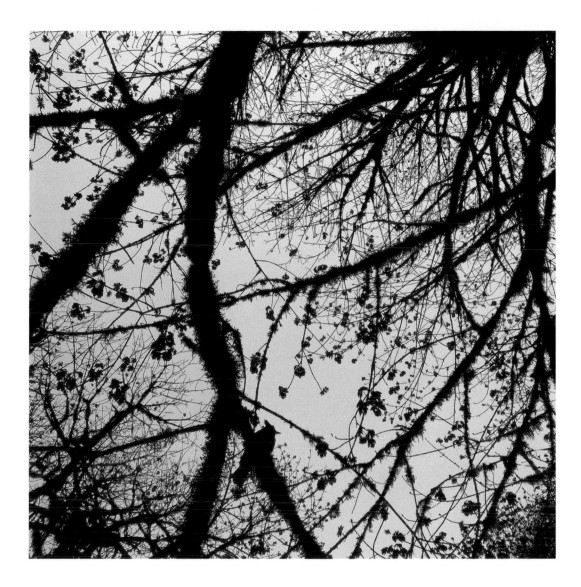

Facing page: Streambank arnica
along the Ohanapecosh River,
Washington

Above: Steller's jay, Redwood
National Park, northern
California

Overleaf: Moss-draped cedar,
Sydney River, Clayoquot Sound,
British Columbia

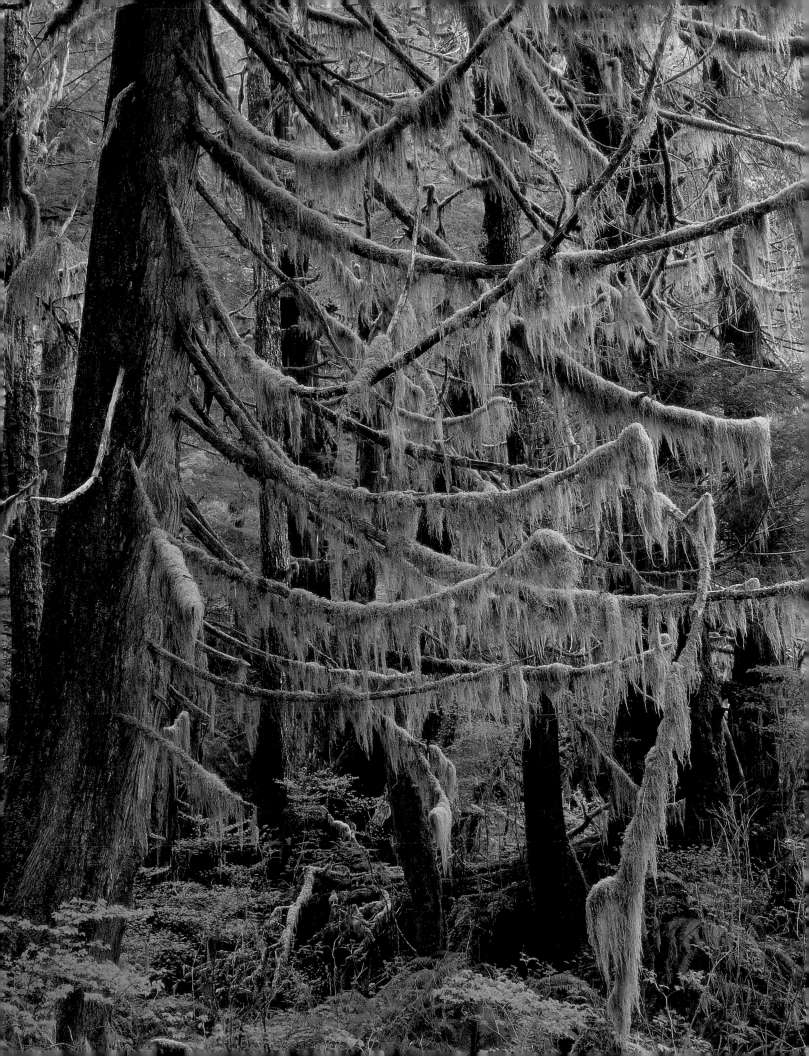

Moss and ferns,
  and leaves and twigs, light and air,
 depth and colour chattering,
   dancing a mad joy-dance,
       but only apparently tied up in stillness and silence.

Emily Carr, *Hundreds and Thousands*

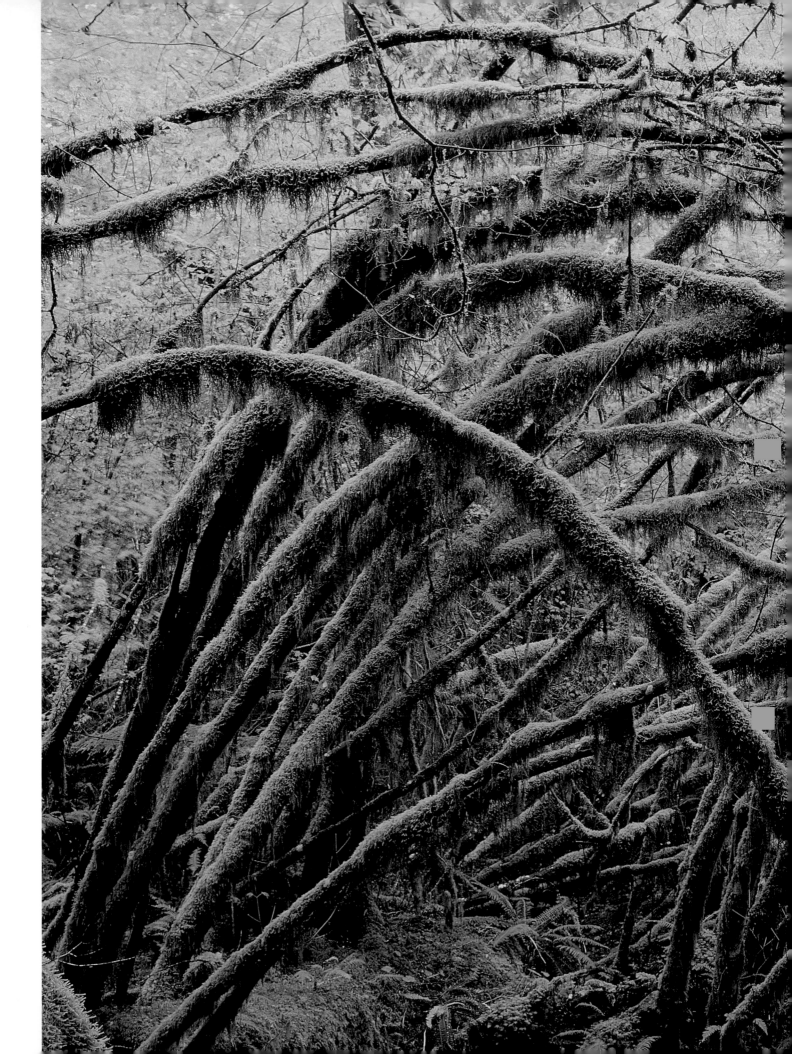

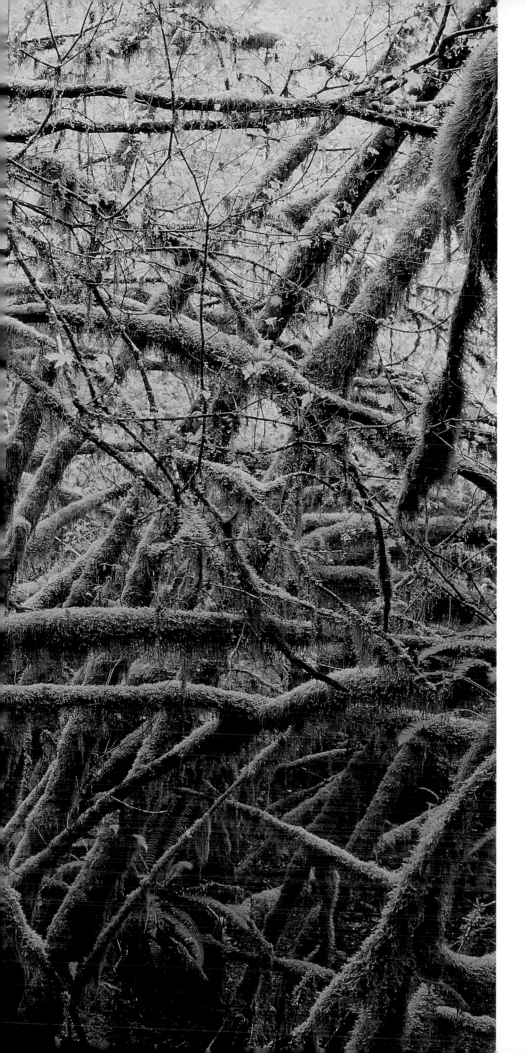

Vine maples, Carbon River,
Washington

Overleaf: Backlit moss, Del
Norte Coast Redwoods State
Park, northern California

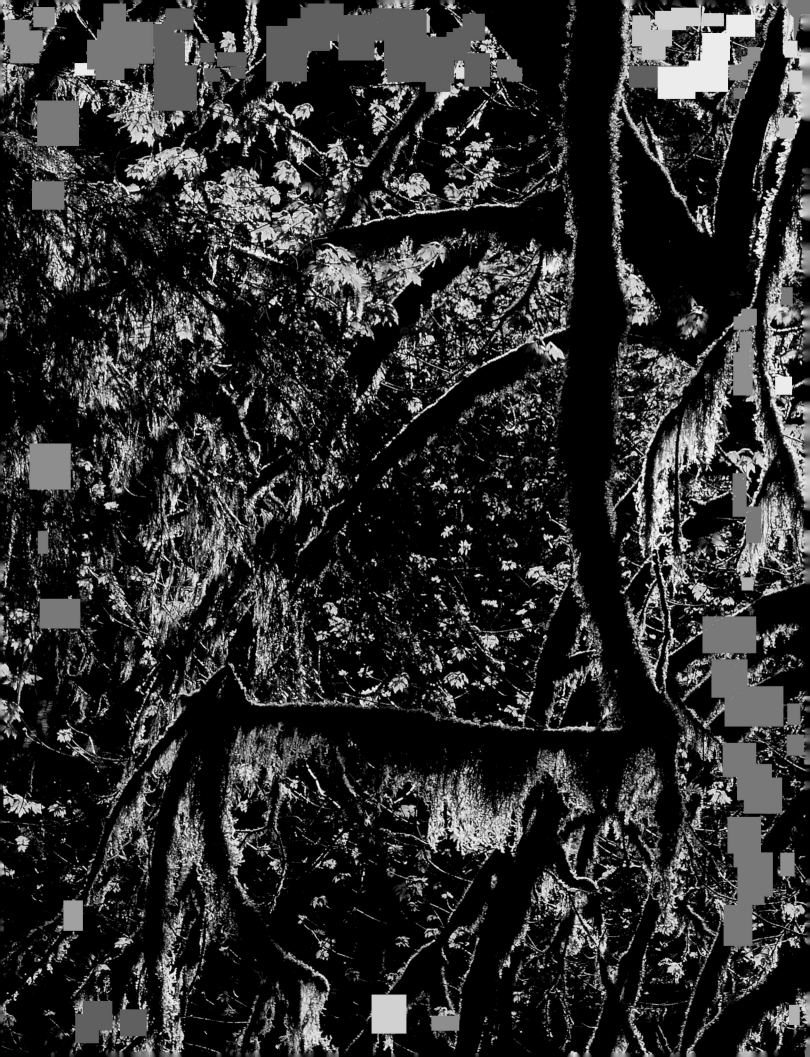

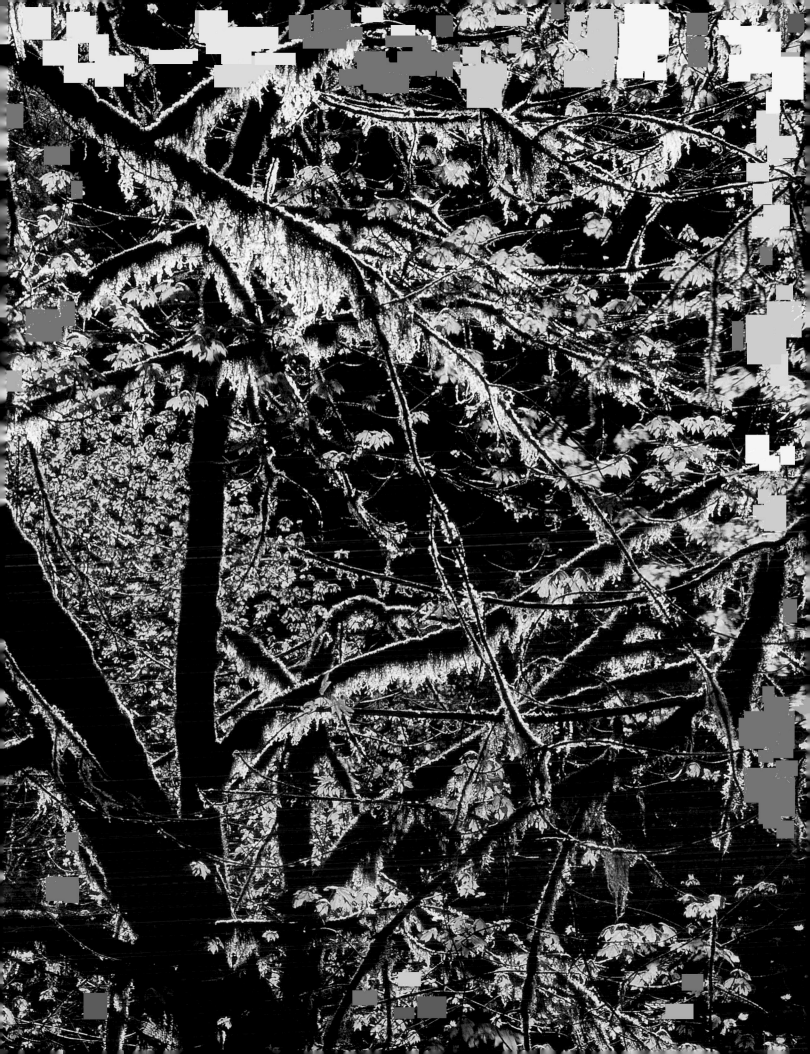

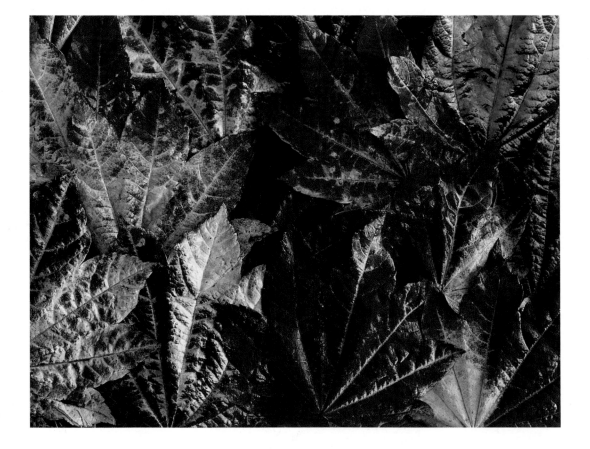

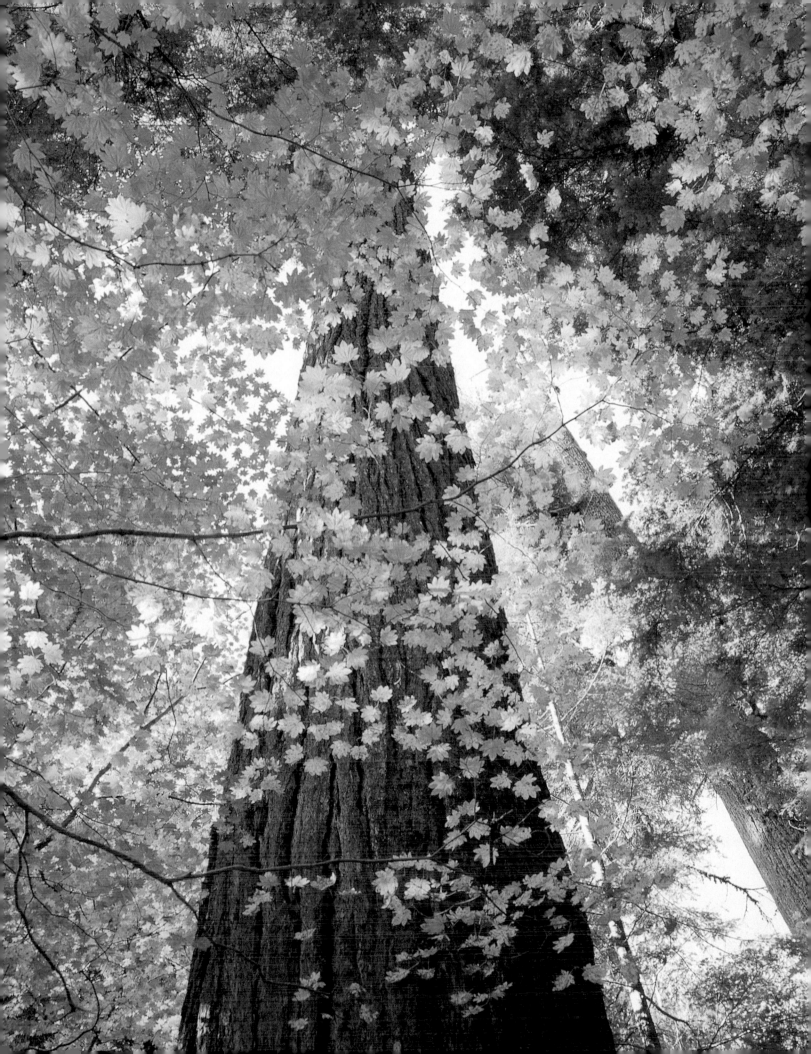

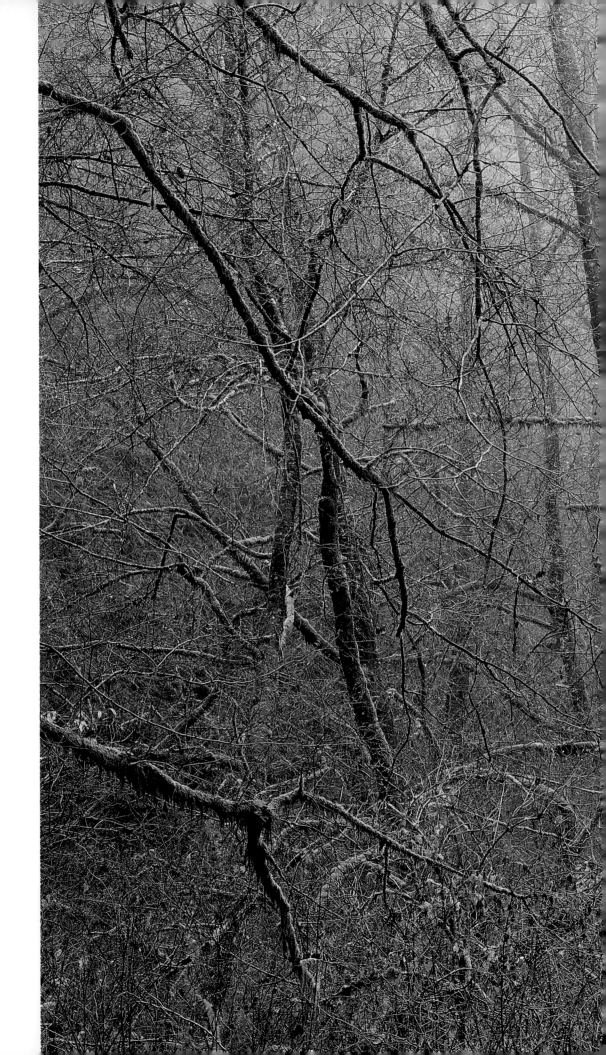

Ancient redwood snag,
Redwood National Park,
northern California

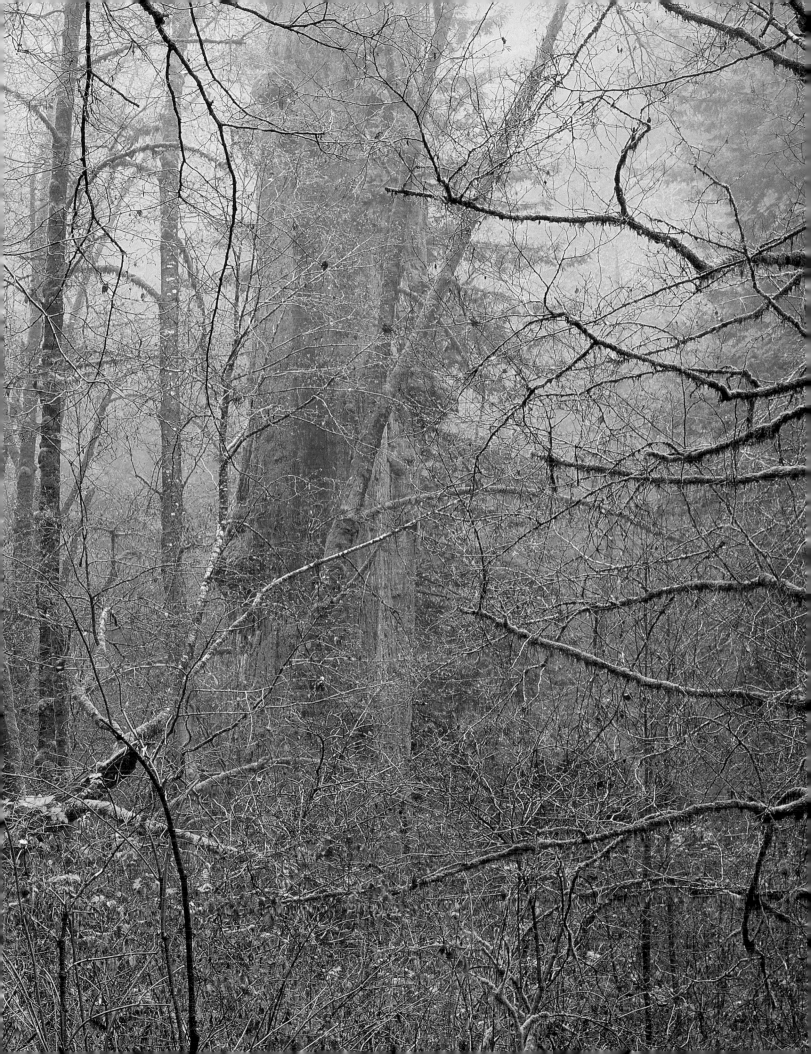

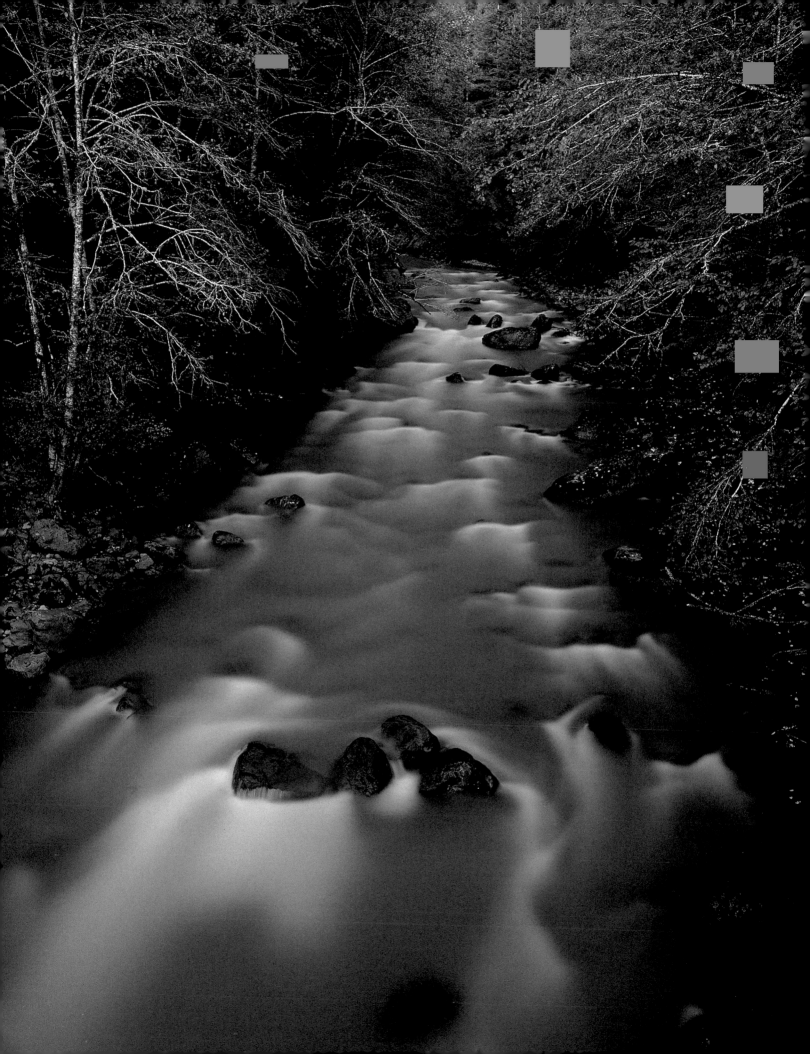

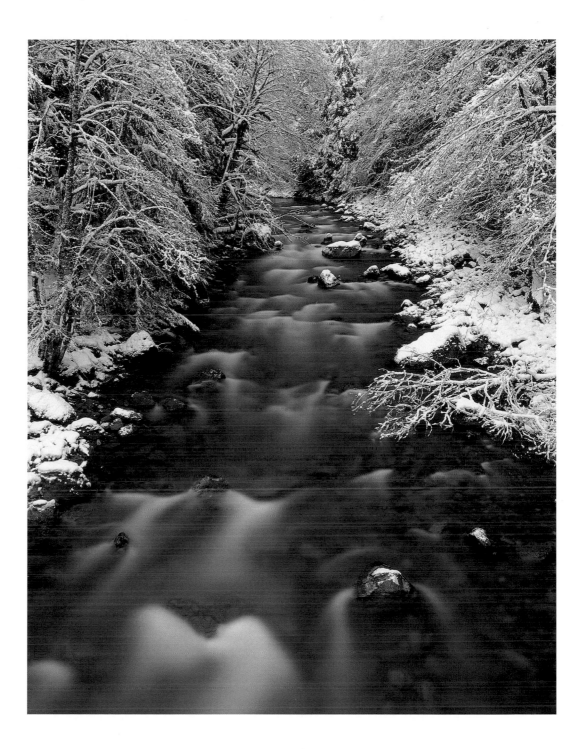

Facing page: Fall, north fork of the Nooksack River, Mt. Baker– Snoqualmie National Forest, Washington

Above: Winter, north fork of the Nooksack River, Mt. Baker– Snoqualmie National Forest, Washington

Overleaf: Silver thaw, Fraser Valley, British Columbia

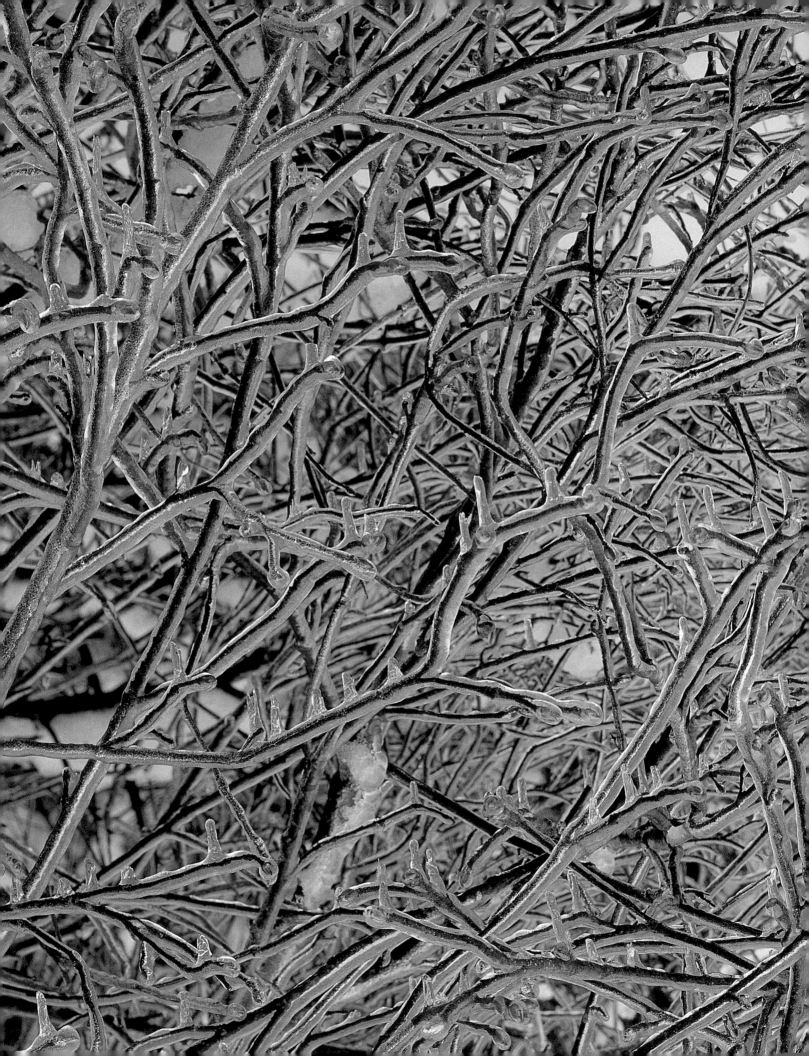

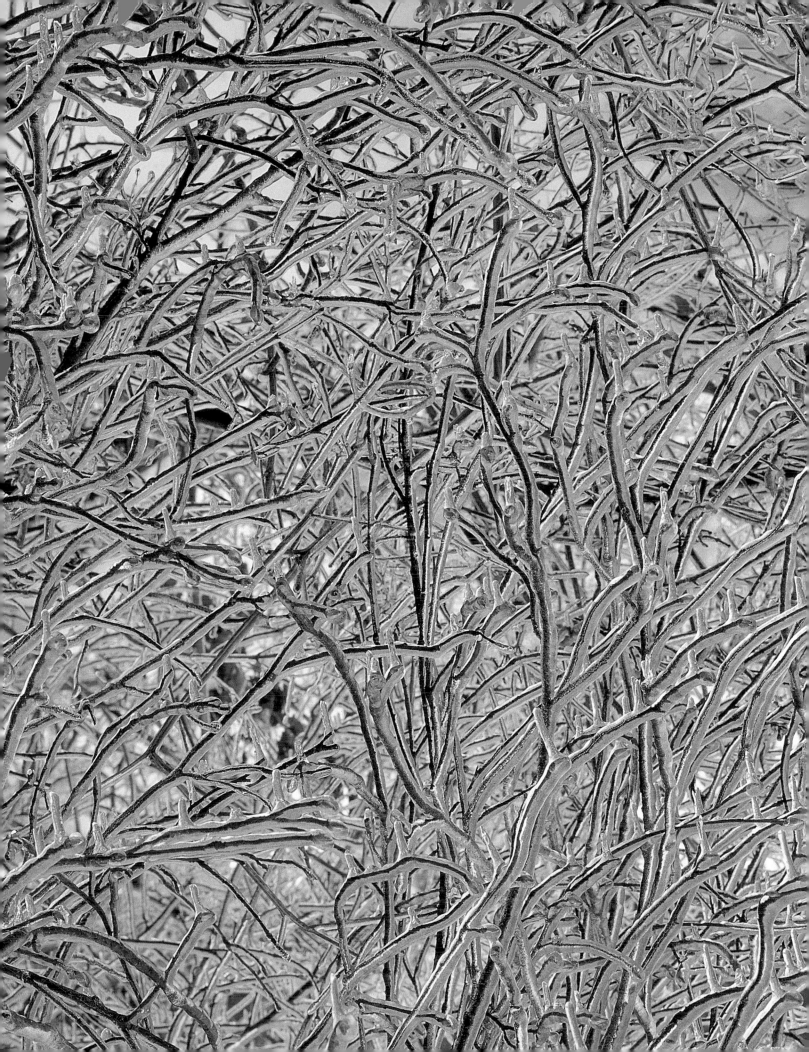

*Below: Ice-encrusted ferns,
Chehalis River, British Columbia*

*Right: Nooksack Canyon in
snow, Mt. Baker–Snoqualmie
National Forest, Washington*

*Following page: Grove of giant
western red cedars, Clayoquot
Valley, British Columbia*

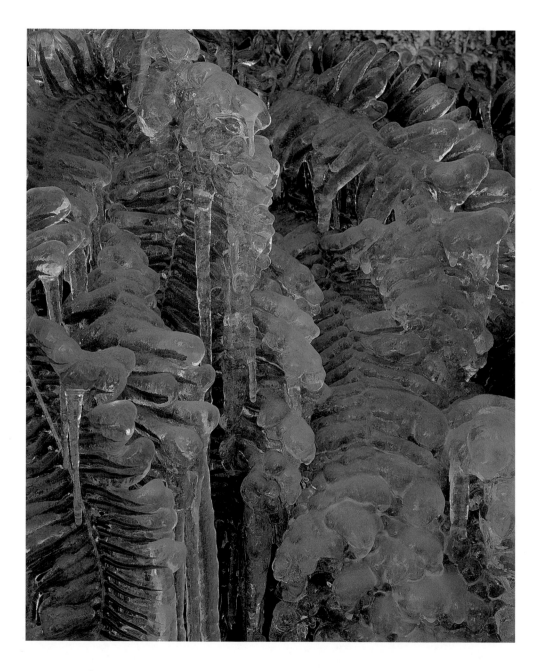

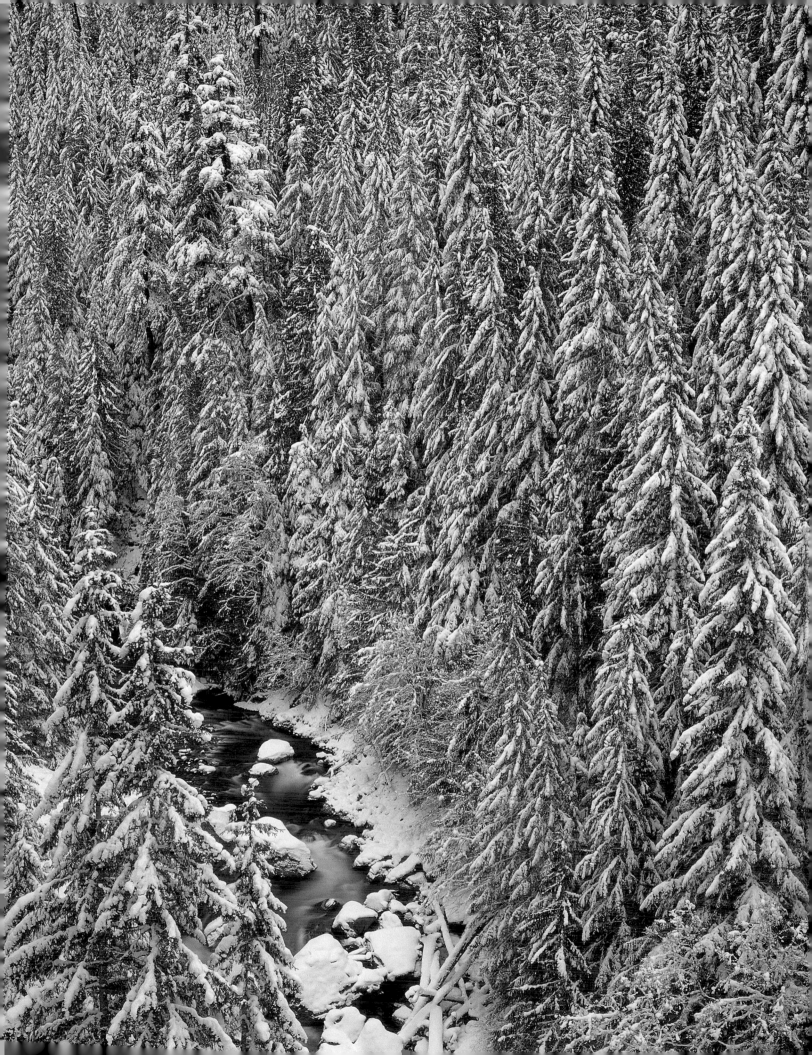

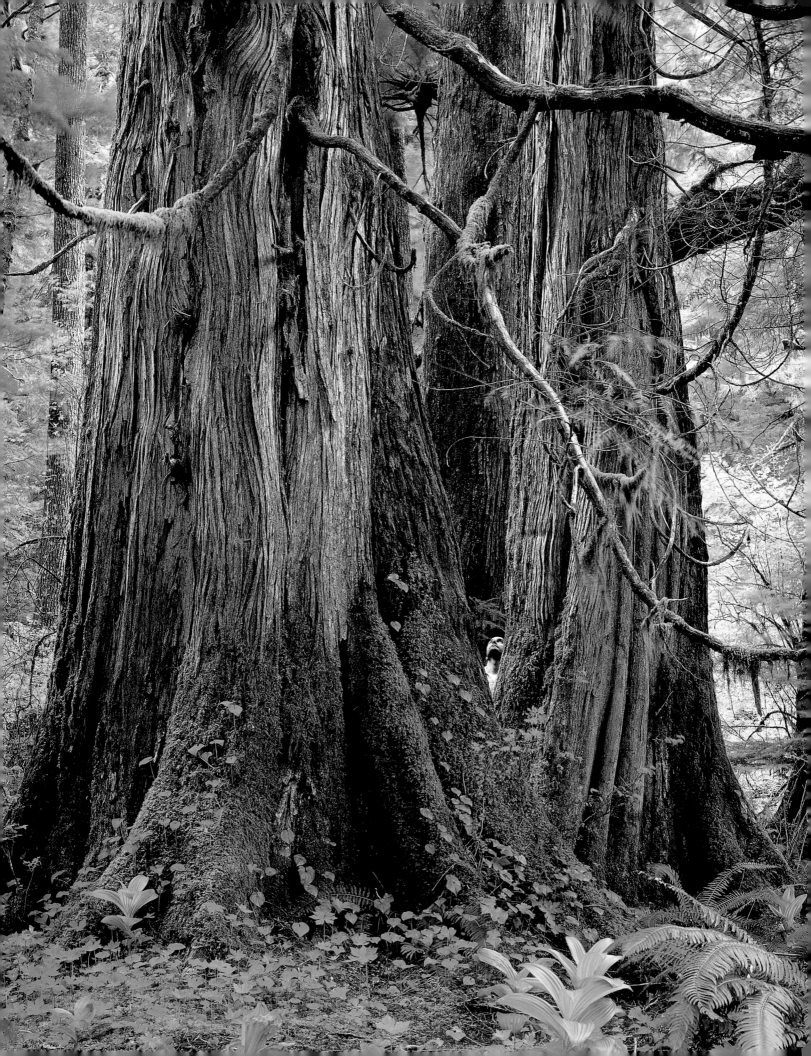

Hear the roaring vastness

of a great valley, or the sigh of wind in the treetops,

or the eternal thunder of breakers on the shore.

Then go back and speak to the world from your heart.

Randy Stoltmann, Heaven Grove Memorial, Carmanah Pacific Provincial Park

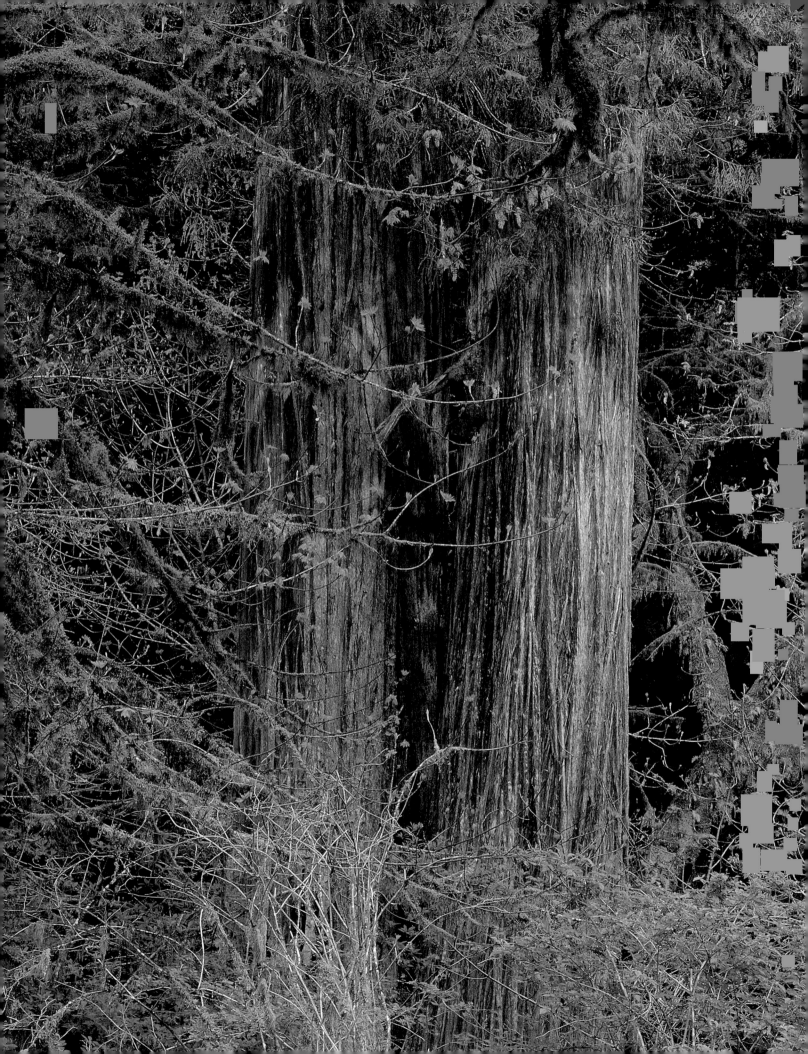

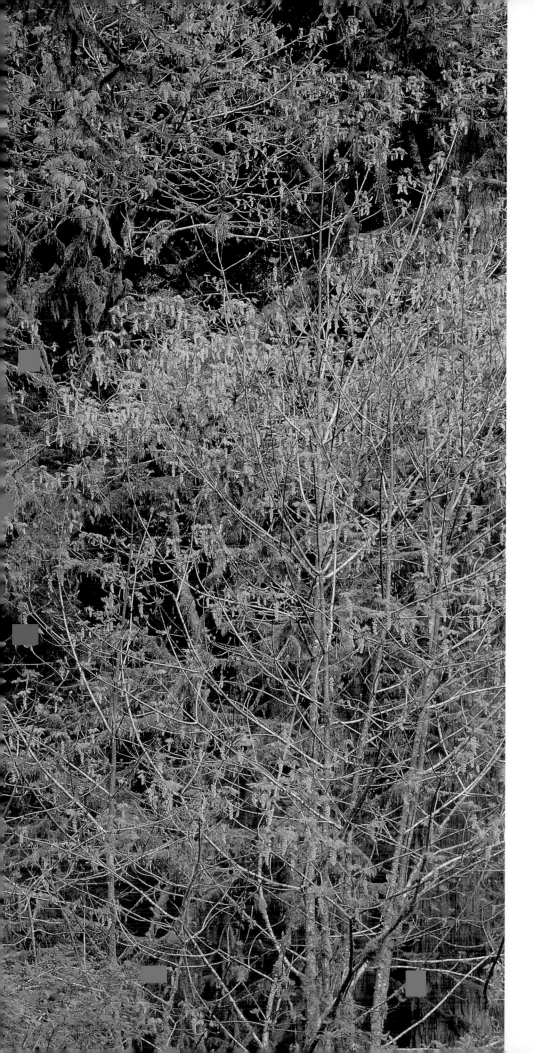

*Coast redwoods, Prairie Creek
Redwoods State Park, northern
California*

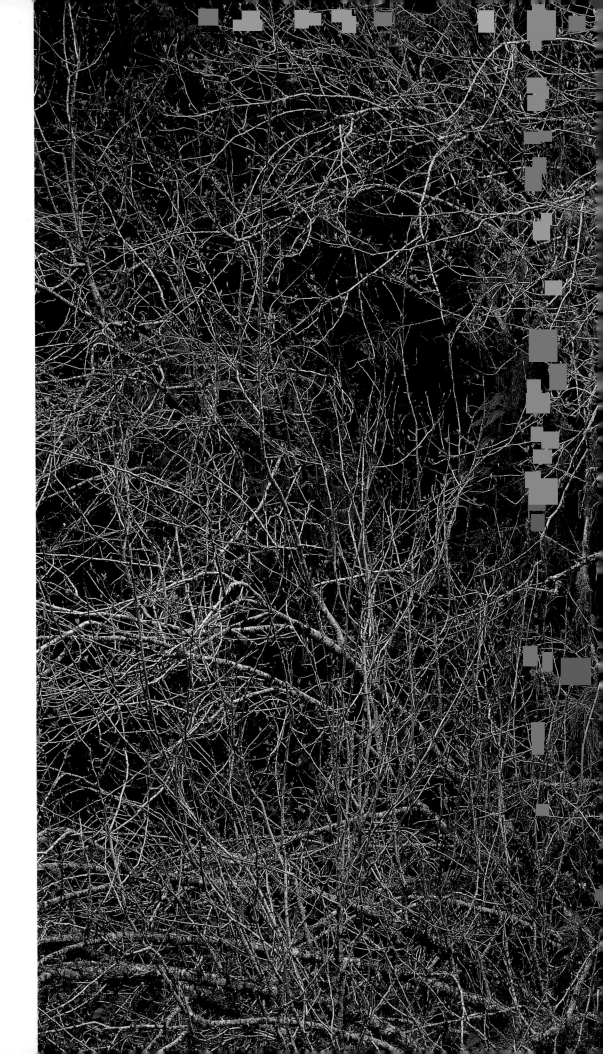

Branches patterned with moss and lichen, Sydney River, Clayoquot Sound, British Columbia

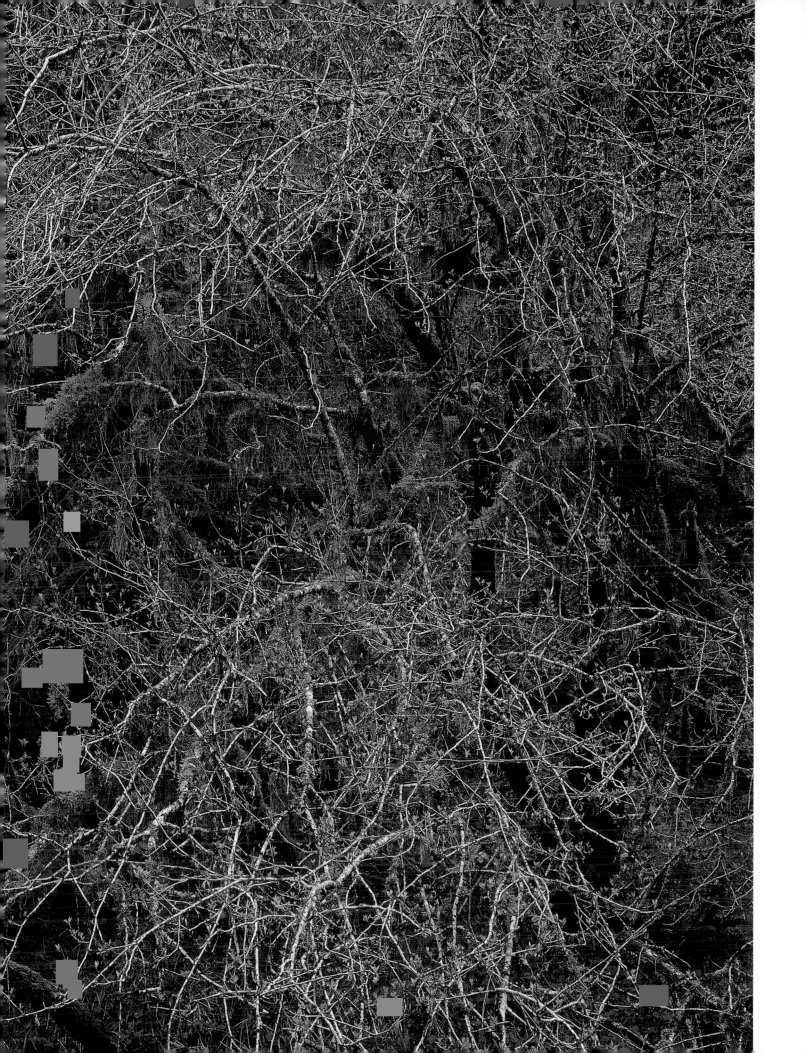

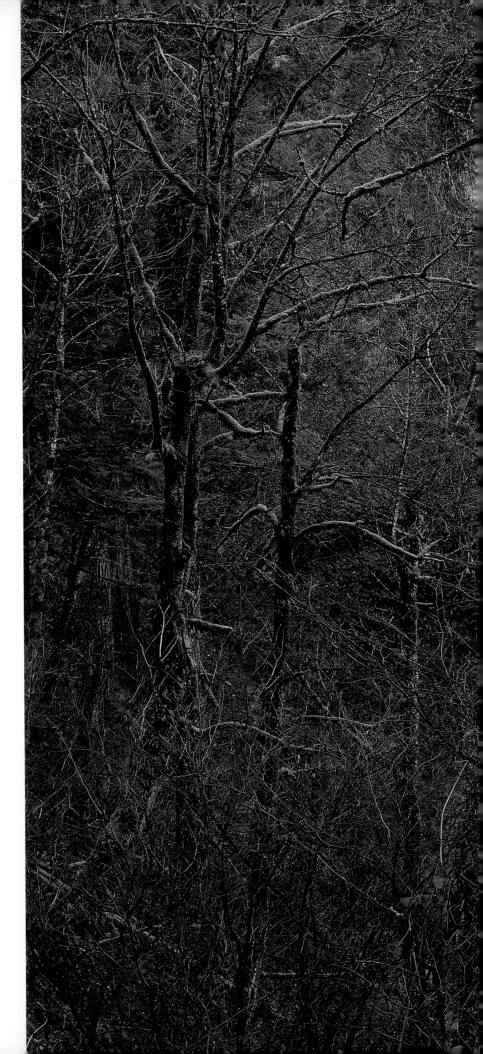

Waterfall, Columbia River
gorge, Oregon

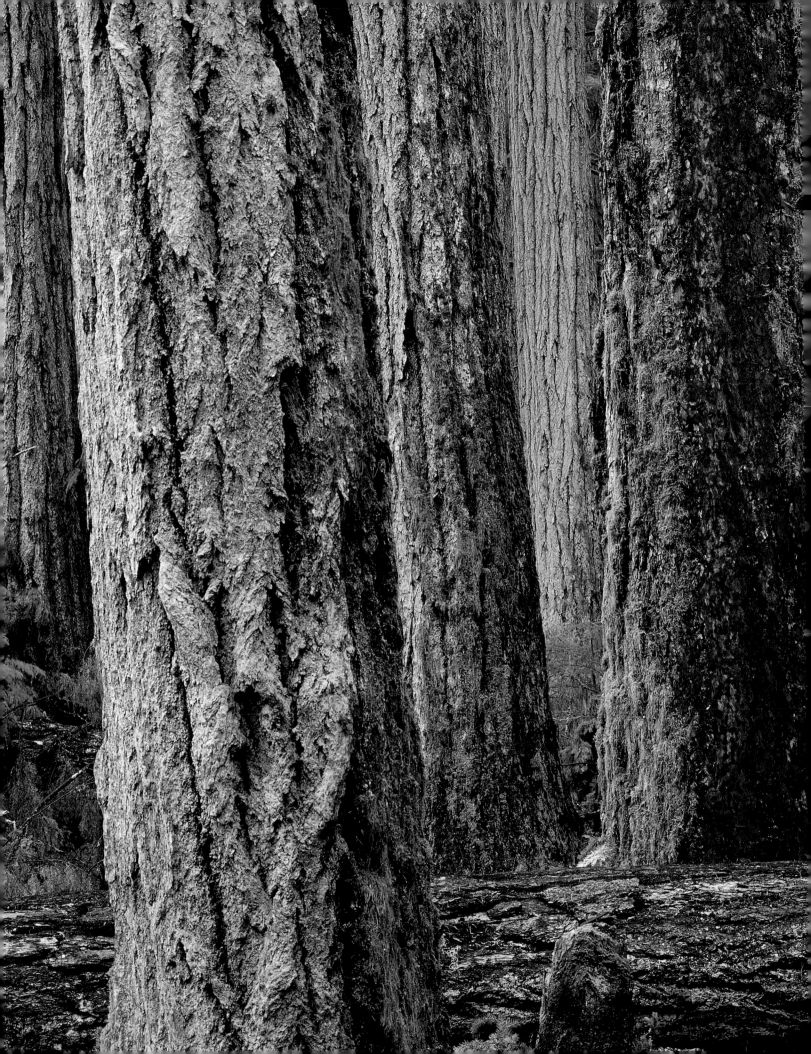

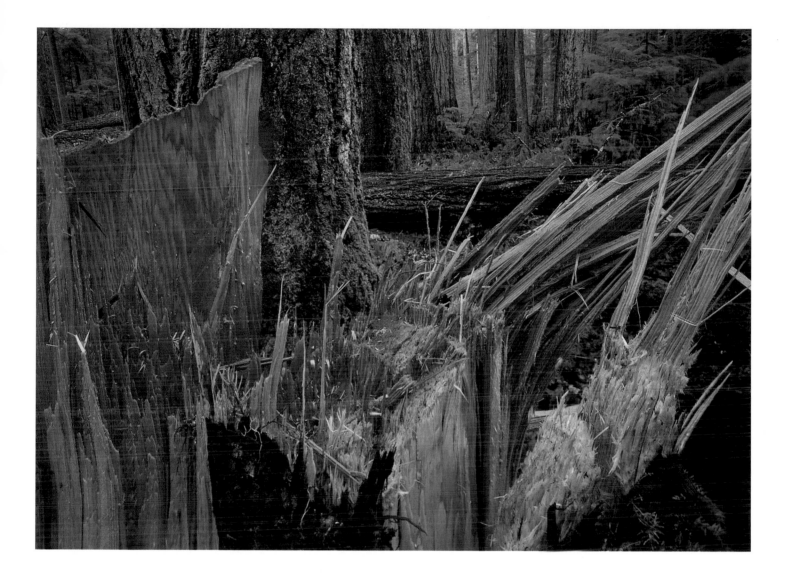

Facing page: Massive stand of
Douglas fir in Cathedral Grove,
MacMillan Provincial Park,
British Columbia

Above: Shattered butt of a giant
Douglas fir blowdown,
Cathedral Grove, MacMillan
Provincial Park, British
Columbia

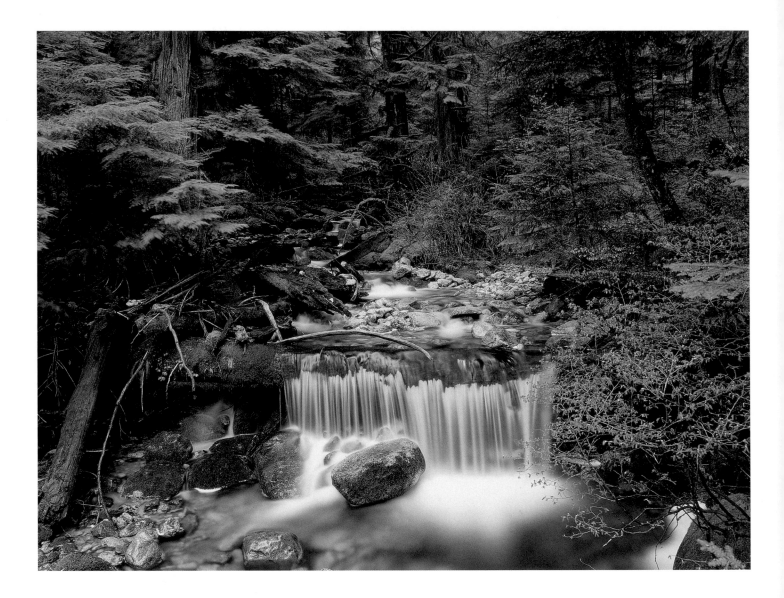

Above: Waterfall, Coquitlam watershed near Vancouver, British Columbia

Facing page: Waterfall, Ellerslie Valley, midcoast of British Columbia

Following page: Pinder Peak, northern Vancouver Island, British Columbia

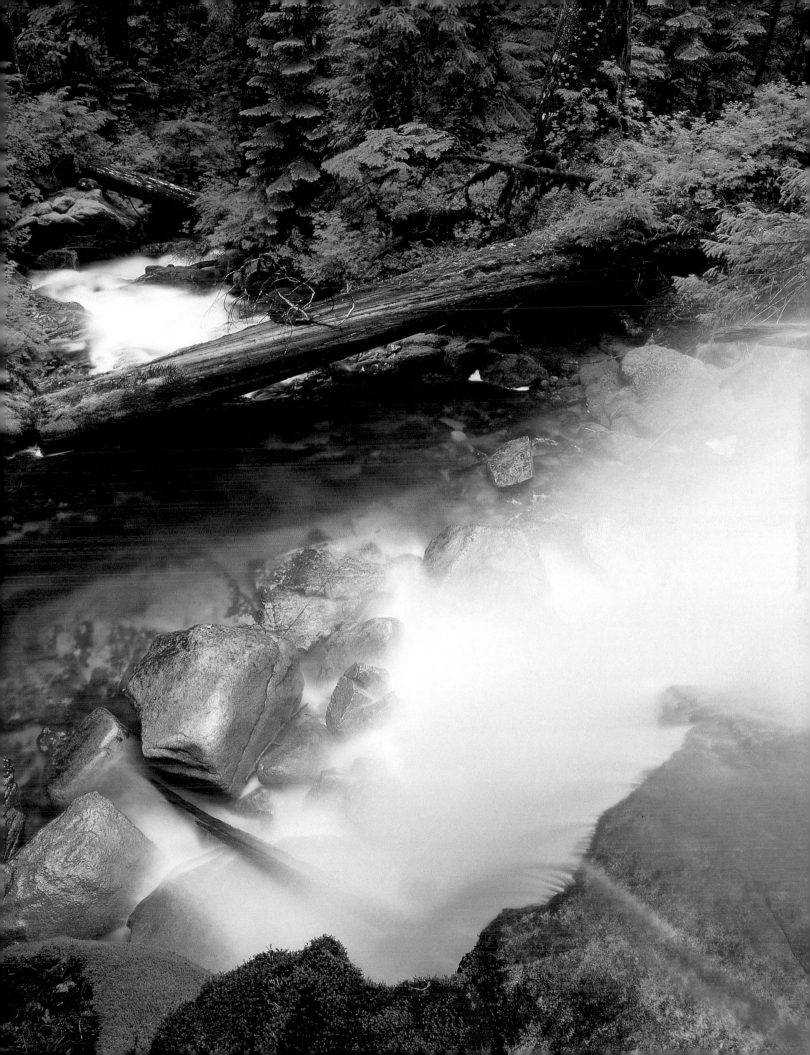

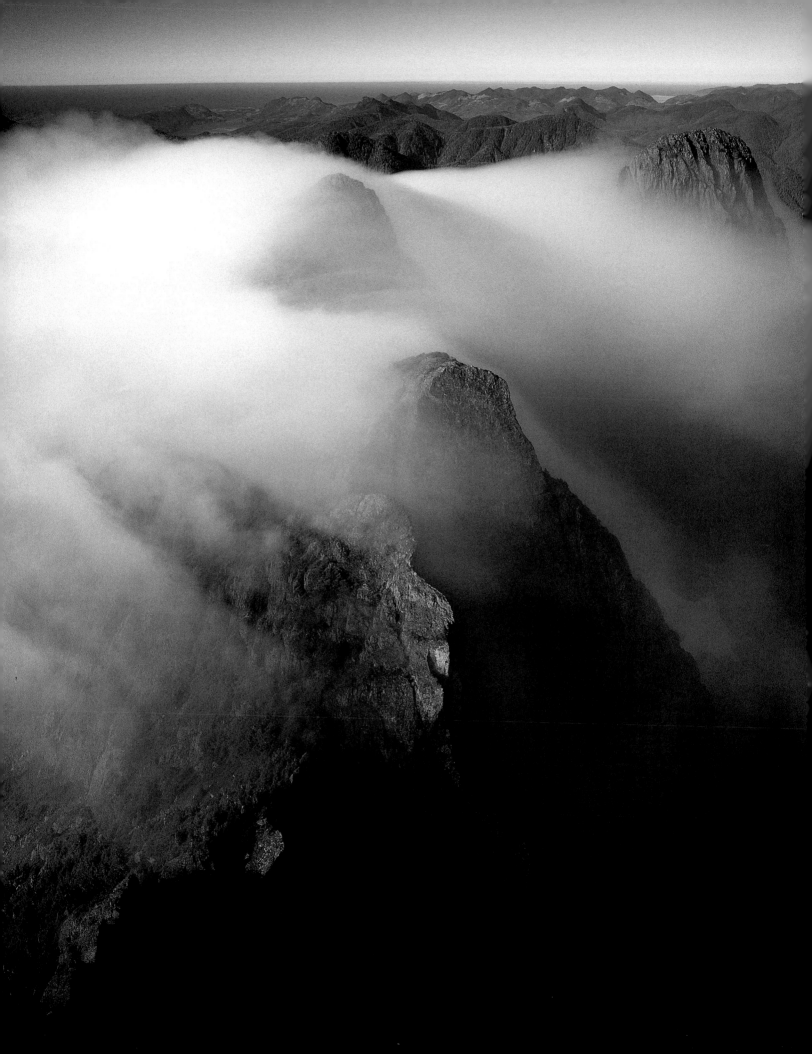

Here is temple music,

the very heart-gladness

of the earth going on forever.

John Muir, *John of the Mountains: The Unpublished Journals of John Muir*

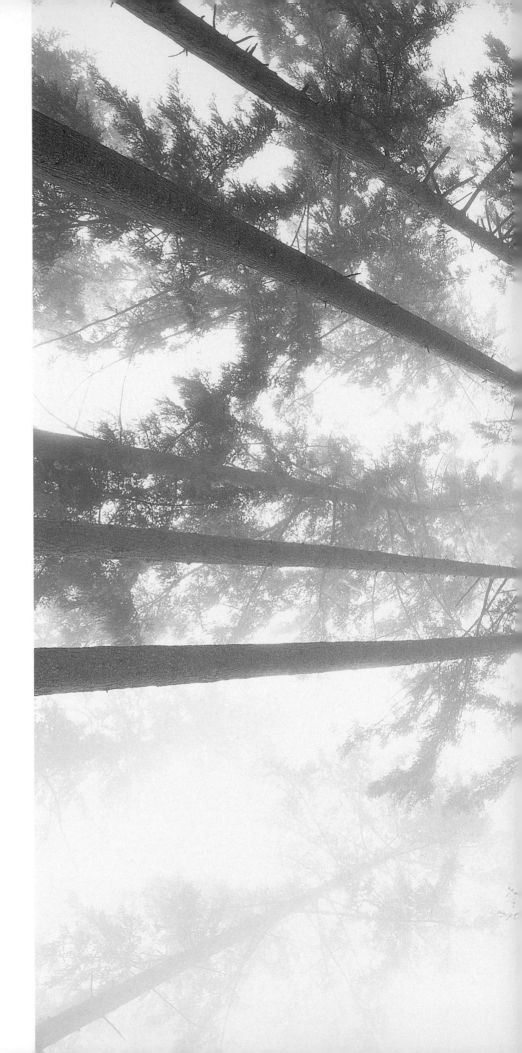

Douglas fir stand near the
Rogue River, Oregon

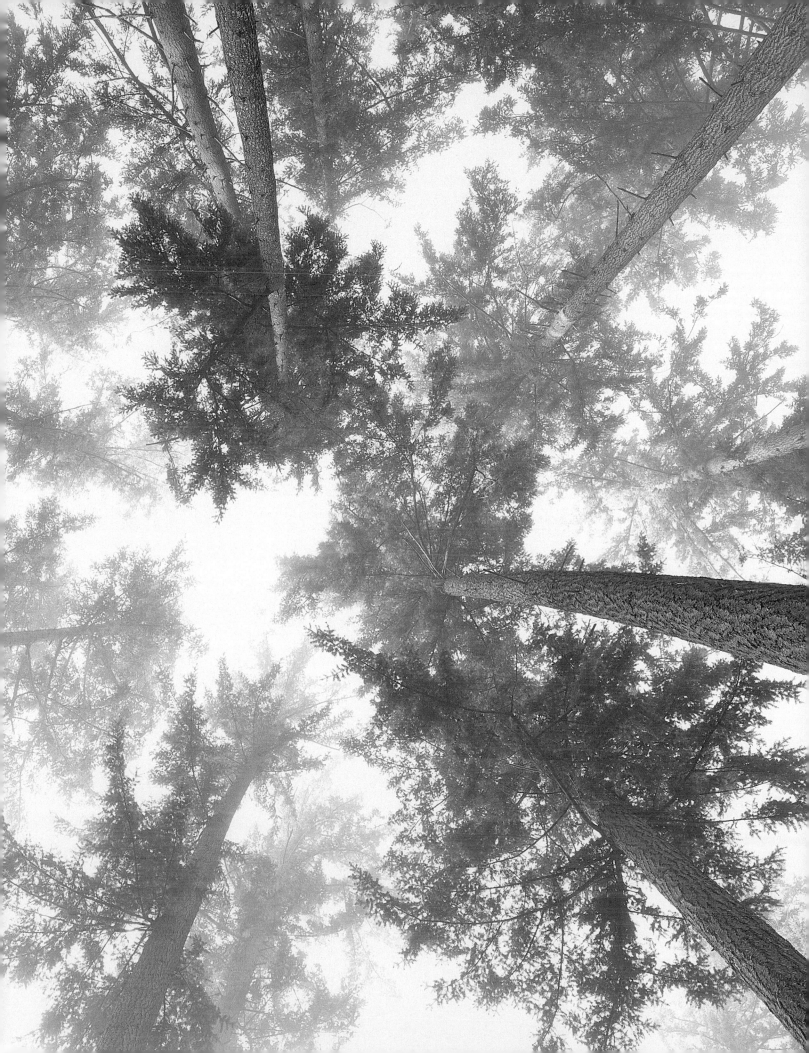

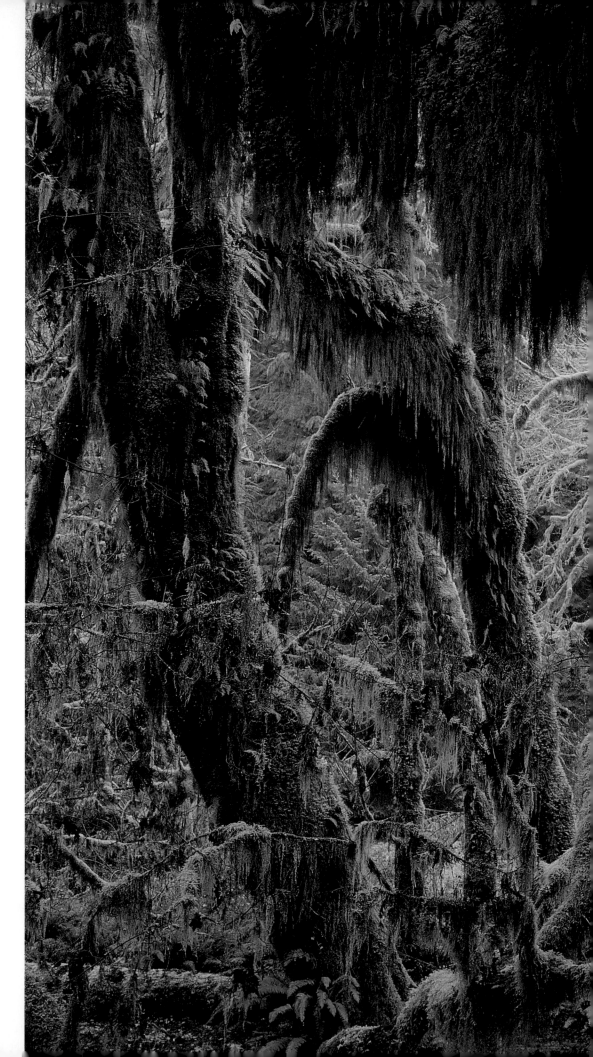

Big leaf maples, Hall of Mosses,
Olympic National Park,
Washington

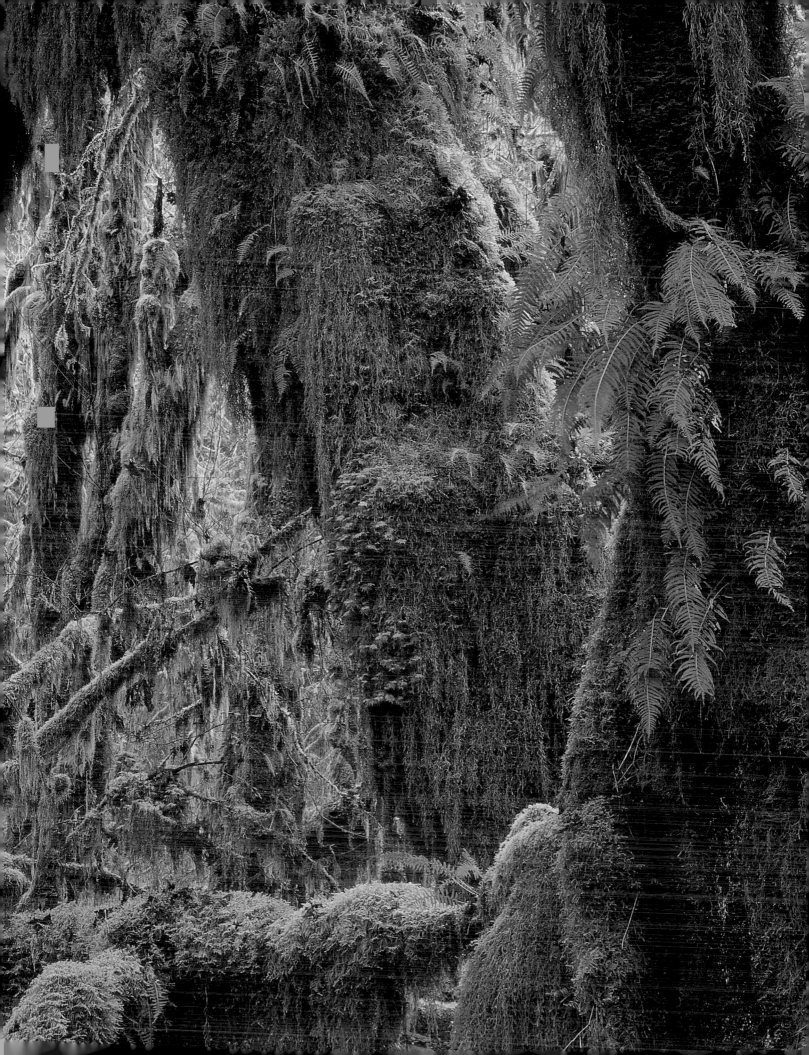

Below: Western red cedars with old-growth candelabras at dusk, Pacific Rim National Park, Vancouver Island, British Columbia

Facing page: Moonrise and marine fog over the Tahsis Valley near Woss Lake, British Columbia

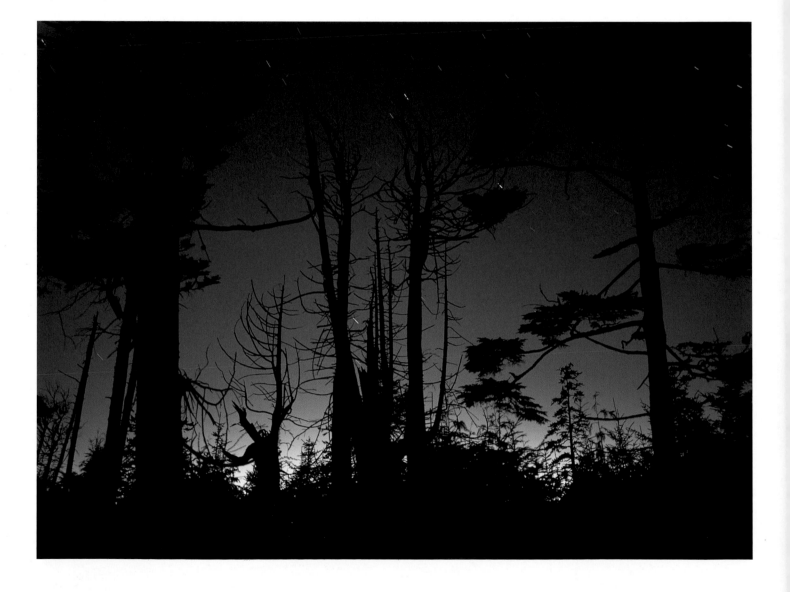

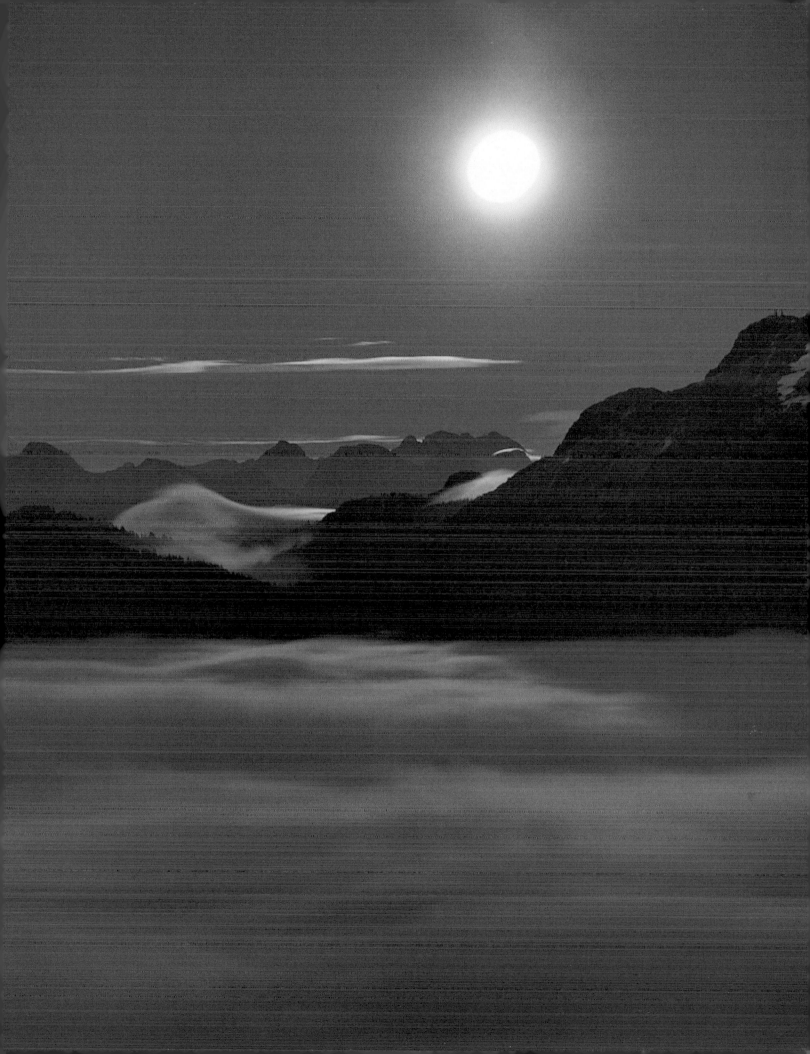

Moonrise with cirrus cloud halo, Stoltmann Wilderness, British Columbia

Acknowledgements

A special thanks to my mum and dad, Rose and Ken Osborne, and my grandma, Rozalia Garbiar, for their love and unwavering support over the years. And to Myrna Colwill for her love, friendship and support and the long hours spent helping me put all aspects of this book together. Many of the images in this book are dedicated to her in my heart.

Many other people were of great help in the assembling of this book, and their efforts are much appreciated. Thanks to Paul Good of Custom Color Lab for unparallelled E6 processing and attention to detail, and to Steve Good, Mike, Julie, Kim, Ian, Tina, Chris and Richard, who all help make this the best photo lab in the province; Wade Davis for his exceptional text and vision; Rob Sanders, my publisher at Greystone/Douglas & McIntyre for his great support of my photography, and Nancy Flight and all the staff at Greystone/ Douglas & McIntyre for helping make this book possible; George Vaitkunas for great design; David McQueen and the staff at Pentax Canada for exceptional pro support and equipment loans; the staff at Leo's Cameras for great technical support; Wayne and Joanne Finn, Tim Briggs and all the crew at West Coast Helicopter in Port McNeill for spectacular flights over Vancouver Island and the mainland coast; Sven Johannsen (North Star of Herschel Island) for expert skippering through the midcoast of British Columbia on several occasions; Rupert Wong for expert guiding in Kyuquot Sound; Jim Laggey, my pilot in the Ellerslie Valley, who was killed in a plane crash along with four other people shortly after dropping me off; Paul George, Adriane Carr, Joe Foy, Sue Fox and the staff at the Western Canada Wilderness Committee for their technical support and encouragement; Peter McCallister for organizing several trips up the midcoast of British Columbia; Susan and Mike Jones for their great Tofino hospitality and help; Richard Cannings for expert caption debugging; Cheech, my adopted dog and travelling buddy; and my good friends John Banovic and Chris Kielesinski for their no-survivors road trip accompaniment.

Wade Davis would like to thank Sharon and Jay Rockefeller, Simon Davies, Cindy Davies, Herb Hammond, Richard Cannings, Ian Gill, the men and women of Dinan Bay, and Gail Percy.

The quotations in this book are from the following sources:

Page 47: Ruth Kirk, "What Is the Rain Forest?" in *The Olympic Rain Forest* (Seattle: University of Washington Press, 1966), p. 3.

Page 55: Gerry Ellis and Karen Kane, "An Evergreen Oasis," *America's Rain Forest* (Minocqua, Wis.: NorthWord Press, 1991), p. 107.

Page 65: Timothy Egan, *The Good Rain: Across Time and Terrain in the Pacific Northwest* (New York: A Borzoi Book/Knopf, 1990), p. 39.

Page 71: Paul Alaback and Jim Pojar, "Vegetation from Ridgetop to Seashore," in *The Rain Forests of Home: Profile of a North American Bioregion*, ed. Peter K. Schoonmaker, Bettina von Hagen and Edward C. Wolf (Washington, D.C.: Island Press, 1997), p. 69.

Page 83: Gerry Ellis and Karen Kane, "The Forest and the Trees," *America's Rain Forest* (Minocqua, Wis.: NorthWord Press, 1991), p. 32.

Page 91: Emily Carr, *Hundreds and Thousands, The Emily Carr Omnibus* (Vancouver: Douglas & McIntyre; Seattle: University of Washington Press, 1993), p. 794.

Page 119: John Muir, *John of the Mountains: The Unpublished Journals of John Muir* (Boston: Houghton Mifflin, 1938), p. 233.

Technical Notes

The images in this book were shot predominantly with medium- and large-format cameras. A Toyo 45A 4×5 camera was used extensively, along with 47, 90 and 150 mm lenses. A Pentax 67 camera was also used for many images, along with 45, 55, 90 and 200 mm lenses, and has proved to be a superb field camera. Nikon 35 mm equipment was used for most wildlife and long telephoto shots, including an 80 mm–200 mm zoom lens and a 600 mm telephoto lens.

Fuji Velvia transparency film was used for most images in the book because of its excellent colour saturation throughout the spectrum and its particularly rich greens. Kodak Ektachrome Lumiere 100x was used pushed one stop for several images in the book because of its speed and warm, lush rendering of rainforest greens. Fuji Provia 100 was also used where greater film speed was needed.

A Manfrotto 055 tripod, ball head and cable release were used for most shots, as well as a Minolta Autometer III incident light meter for determining exposure. Other equipment included an underwater housing, lens shades and a stopwatch for longer exposures. A polarizing filter was used to remove reflections and saturate colours in some shots, and an 81A or 81B filter was used to correct for excessive film sensitivity to blue light in some circumstances, particularly during dawn, dusk, blue skies and long exposures.